D0200167

Advance Praise for *The Other Game*

"From first inspiring page to the last, the authors give us the politics of hope. Found in the indigenous communities of Mexico's southern mountains, this is a gift of enduring wisdom. Read these pages filled with enthusiasm and conviction, and start playing the game of sustainable, balanced life."

—Tom Barry, author of *Zapata's Revenge:*
Free Trade and the Farm Crisis in Mexico

"The wisdom of these well-tested, sometimes reclaimed, traditional practices enables these communities to play a leadership role in the urgent search for life-support for our planet and her people. They are role models for us."

—Marie Dennis, co-president of Pax Christi International
and director of the Maryknoll Office for Global Concerns
in Washington, D.C.

"We are all—nations as well as individuals—understandably trapped inside of our own 'game,' but there are ways out! The ideas and practices blossoming in these small communities can lead us all to a bigger, more inclusive, and surely much better world."

—Richard Rohr, author of *Everything Belongs*

The authors have assigned all royalties generated by the sale of this book to support the work of CEDICAM and other projects in Oaxaca that strengthen indigenous culture and practice.

THE OTHER GAME

*Lessons from How Life Is Played
in Mexican Villages*

PHIL DAHL-BREDINE
————— AND —————
STEPHEN HICKEN

ORBIS BOOKS

Maryknoll, New York 10545

Founded in 1970, Orbis Books endeavors to publish works that enlighten the mind, nourish the spirit, and challenge the conscience. The publishing arm of the Maryknoll Fathers and Brothers, Orbis seeks to explore the global dimensions of the Christian faith and mission, to invite dialogue with diverse cultures and religious traditions, and to serve the cause of reconciliation and peace. The books published reflect the views of their authors and do not represent the official position of the Maryknoll Society. To learn more about Maryknoll and Orbis Books, please visit our website at www.maryknoll.org.

Copyright © 2008 by Phil Dahl-Bredine and Stephen Hicken.

Published by Orbis Books, Maryknoll, NY 10545-0308.

All rights reserved.

No part of this publication may be reproduced or transmitted in any form or by any means, electronic or mechanical, including photocopying, recording, or any information storage or retrieval system, without prior permission in writing from the publisher.

Queries regarding rights and permissions should be addressed to Orbis Books, P.O. Box 308, Maryknoll, NY 10545-0308.

Manufactured in the United States of America.

Library of Congress Cataloging-in-Publication Data   .
Dahl-Bredine, Phil, and Stephen Hicken.
    The other game : lessons from how life is played in Mexican villages /
Phil Dahl-Bredine and Stephen Hicken.
        p.   cm.
    ISBN 978-1-57075-780-8
    1. Mixtec Indians – History. 2. Mixtec Indians – Social life and customs.
    I. Hicken, Stephen K., 1956-   II. Title.
F1221.M7D28 2008
972.00497′63 – dc22

                                                                2007038900

We dedicate this book to the campesino people of
the Center for Integral Campesino Development of the Mixteca,
who have chosen to change their universe instead of
living with environmental catastrophe and poverty:
Jesús Pacheco, Adelina Santiago, Enrique López,
Jesús León, Fermina Zárate, Pedro Velasco, Eleazar García,
Anastacia Velasco, Aaron Santiago, Fidel Cruz, Pablo Jiménez,
Alfonso López, Josefina Jiménez, and Fidelia Santiago.

May they inspire us to do likewise.

It is also dedicated to Don Aurelio
and the people of Santiago Ixtayutla,
who to this day struggle against the manipulations
and violence of the reigning political powers
of the state of Oaxaca.

May they give us courage to commit ourselves
to the magnitude of change that we will need for the work
of renewing the planet politically and environmentally.

Contents

Part I
LEAVING BEHIND THE U.S. CULTURAL
AND MORAL BORDER

Part II
ANCIENT ALIEN VALUES

Part III
LEARNING HOPE

12. Happiness and a Sustainable World
    *How Can We Respond to the Invitation of Indigenous
    Peoples and the Global South?* 134

Preface

The Other Game grows out of a deep and unexpected personal encounter with people from an indigenous culture in the Mixteca Alta of the state of Oaxaca in southern Mexico. People such as Fermina Zarate, Jesús León, Fidel Cruz, Jesús Pacheco, Pablo Jiménez, Agustín León, and Josefina Jiménez have become friends and discussion partners during the last six years. These friendships form the foundation for this book, which centers on the Mixtec culture as a foil or a looking glass through which to observe our own Western ways, presuppositions, and basic commitments. To share this experience we will go to indigenous villages, to street demonstrations, to homes and organizing meetings of workers, small farmers, and nonprofit organizations around Mexico and South America.

In the pages that follow, we do not approach indigenous society and civilization as archeologists or anthropologists, which we are not. Nor do we focus on the spirituality of indigenous cultures, which have always revered and retained close communication with Mother Earth. In this book, we concern ourselves with how Mixtecs live out their basic social, spiritual, philosophical, and economic presuppositions, and we examine how their way of life presents concrete alternatives to the dominant Western culture or the American Way of Life that we must take seriously in order to create a sustainable future for ourselves, our human race, and the other dwellers on the planet. We argue the unusual thesis that, far from being dead archaeological phenomena, far from being romanticized throwbacks to a lost paradise, these indigenous societies present strong contemporary options.

We think we should forewarn the reader here. These pages present much more than a mere collection of interesting experiences with the Mixtec people of Oaxaca. Rather, what we learned from these people came to be a direct challenge to a lifestyle and a worldview that recent U.S. political leaders have identified as the American Way of Life. This worldview and lifestyle exalts unrestrained accumulation and resource use, both individual and corporate. It justifies the privatization of the world's resources in the hands of those who already control the lion's share of those resources and is willing to defend the right to that lion's share, our share, with the force of regressive laws, concentration of political and economic power in the hands of individual and corporate elites, and, ultimately, through war against the world's poorer majorities.

We pass on this challenge to this American Way of Life not from malice toward America. Precisely the contrary, we believe that our people and nation have a great deal to contribute. But we are in agreement with many experts in economics, the environment, and politics when we suggest that this lifestyle and worldview are self-destructive, suicidal, albeit unwittingly. It is suicidal primarily in two ways. First it is suicidal environmentally since it requires a disregard for the natural world, the global environment that sustains all of humanity including those of us from the United States. Our earth offers limited resources and exists in a fragile equilibrium. Our American Way of Life not only contaminates the basic elements on which we depend for life but also overexploits them and creates basic scarcities of clean water, fertile soil, breathable air, and safe sources of food that will bring all of humanity to crisis before the end of the present century.

The gap between rich and poor that this "way of life" makes wider each year creates a second way in which this way of life is suicidal. Nearly one-half of the world's 6 billion people live on less than two dollars a day while the average yearly income of U.S. households is $60,528.[1] To defend this kind of imbalance will surely require continuous U.S. economic and military aggression and will risk countless new 9/11-type threats to U.S. citizens.

This century gives us, all of the human family on this planet, an opportunity. We will be forced by the ecological and social realities we will encounter to recognize that the American Way of Life as characterized by our political leaders, far from being a model for others in the world, is really a dead end. It is environmentally unsustainable and socially provocative to the extreme.

The Human Project

We need to recognize and state the obvious. In spite of what the commercial world, the financial world, often even our educational system, tell us, our purpose on this planet is not to accumulate, to spend, and to acquire. Nor is the mall our natural home. Rather we propose that our human project is to find a way to become, as a species, a positive contributing part of this evolving universe and its mysterious and awe-inspiring processes and directions. Though we may from time to time feel insulted by the low estimation of the human potential forced upon us by a society based on getting and spending money, we also find it difficult to imagine alternatives to this spurious American Way of Life.

With this in mind we try to do two things in this book. First, with the help of the Mixtec peoples we imagine together a different lifestyle and worldview, more challenging, constructive, and sustainable than the one we currently practice. Second, we try to stimulate a dialogue within each one of us individually and as a society about what new role we would like to take in the history of this creative and expanding universe.

To this end, in part 1, we will visit the Mixtec indigenous campesino communities of southern Mexico to allow the Mixtec people to stimulate our thoughts about actual living alternatives upon which to base a society's life and worldview.

In part 2 we will draw close to the indigenous and popular movements that are surging across Latin America, to see if, in the way they frame their own goals for the future, we can find help in re-creating a positive living vision for our own future and our common future as a human family.

Readers may often find themselves asking, "But then what should we do?" We will try to resist answering those questions with too many specific proposals. The dialogue that ought to take place here is much too important and much too complex for simple solutions presented in bullet point fashion. We need to challenge one another to undertake this process as a nation, and for this reason we dare to offer only those principles that we think follow from the experience of the peoples we will visit and who will guide us to examine what we can do to address the global challenge we face. This we will try to do in part 3.

The Other Game

We have come to believe that, in essence, the Mixtec people are and always have been playing a different "game" than that which Western European and American societies have chosen to play. We choose this metaphor of a game because we believe that while the stakes are incredibly high, the game metaphor permits us to "play" with options and consider different "moves" without reference to emotionally charged concepts such as "capitalism," "democracy," "socialism," etc. The life game that the Mixtecs play leads to economic, social, and environmental consequences very different from the results produced by the game we play in the North. Though elements of this way of seeing life reside in our own past, the Mixtec view that we all belong to one human and life community leads them to make environmental and social moves considered inappropriate or unwise in the Northern game.

The twenty-first century poses challenges to the way we do things in the North of an urgency never before faced by Western civilization. Could the Mixtec game be the one we need to play for this century, during which we are bumping up against the environmental limits of the planet and against the limits of the social fabric to sustain the monstrous gap between the minority elite, who are surfeited with goods and resources, and the huge majority of humanity that does not know whether it will eat tomorrow?

This five-thousand-year-old Mixtec culture challenges us and our Western intellectual and cultural history at a time of crisis. We find it gives us hope. We thank the people of the Mixteca whose conversations, customs, and commitments have become this sign of hope for us and who compel us to share this hope with you.

Acknowledgments

After about a week of traveling together on most of the forms of transportation in use today, Phil and I found ourselves on the last leg of a long journey, riding a bus from Mexico City to Oaxaca. Three hours into that six-hour trip, you leave a productive agricultural area and enter the cactus-laden, canyon-cut zone leading into Oaxaca State. I sat on the aisle. Phil related an event in his life. I heard the wisdom while viewing the stark geography of the Mixteca Alta climb slowly into view behind him. I said to Phil, "This is a book! We have to capture and communicate all of these life stories, learnings, experiences we've been talking about on this trip." Phil looked over at me and with a combination of a pause, a nod, and then a full and mischievous grin, he agreed that we should try to tell the story of how the people of Oaxaca have been changing our lives and how they offered hope to us all.

Since that time we have received immeasurable help from a great number of friends and family to bring the book to completion. Our thanks to Dave Carlsen, Fr. Paul La Chance, Dave Kane, Janet Gore, Paul Mitchell, Maria Dahl-Bredine, Andrew Dahl-Bredine, Lexa Jobe, Mary Mallahan Hicken, and Kathy Dahl-Bredine, all of whom helped greatly with editing and revising the final drafts of the book. Our thanks also to Erica Dahl-Bredine, Pat Ross, Helen Jaurequi, Mary Tworek-Hofstetter, Virgil Tworek-Hofstetter, and Dominic Dahl-Bredine for clarifying and correcting the stories in which they were involved. The founders and staff of Services for an Alternative Education, AC (EDUCA), Ana María García, Miguel Ángel Vasques de la Rosa, Marcos Leyva Madrid, Aracely Carbajal all contributed their wisdom. Our thanks also to Maryknoll lay missioner Jean Walsh, who first introduced us to the people and the inspiring work of CEDICAM.

Phil Dahl-Bredine and Stephen Hicken

Invitation

I vividly remember my experience of the Grand Canyon from its North Rim. The National Park Service has constructed a walkway out to a viewpoint situated on a promontory that juts out into the vast open space of the canyon itself. The sun had set, and the light was waning. No wind blew, not even a breeze. I climbed a slight rise above the trail and perched on the head of a needle surrounded on all sides by a sea of nothing — and of everything. Silent, still, enormous, the view stretched to infinity.

I felt incredibly small, not even a grain of sand on a beach, a mere speck in the universe.

Some years have passed since that penetrating experience, and I return to the memory because something about it has always seemed incongruous, something didn't "fit." The Grand Canyon taught me a lesson that, not surprisingly for the Grand Canyon, took some time to form. Paradoxically, the knowledge that my existence did not even reach "speck status" in the universal scheme of reality did not cause me to feel diminished. Rather, the experience brought me peace. In a strange way, the experience has given me a sense of arrival and even of relief. The North Rim of the Grand Canyon revealed to me my place in the scheme of things, small and tiny but grounded, authentic, true, a role neither grandiose nor inconsequential. I counted in creation, and it invited me to participate as I truly am, neither larger nor smaller.

This experience serves as a metaphor for this book. As we humans, individuals and communities and nations, create self-images that are neither inflated nor diminished, we become liberated to participate in the global project of nurturing life — all life. Our actions become more effective. We "feel" balanced, in harmony, and that we are about our purpose.

Mexican author Francisco Martín Moreno, writing about U.S. president James Polk, who in 1846 prepared to take over the Mexican states of California and New Mexico (including all of what is now called Colorado, New Mexico, Arizona, Utah, Nevada, and California) by purchase, theft, or war, quotes President Polk:.

1

We Americans, we Anglo-Saxons, constitute a superior race destined to take good government, commercial prosperity and good
Christianity to the nations of the world. In our spirit of indus-
triousness there is no room for the unproductive. It is our duty
to those who have fallen into perdition or who have lost their
way to guide them to the world of prosperity, and if necessary, by
force.[1]

Polk's justification for a war that he did indeed successfully carry out
might seem to most of us as a caricature of American racism. U.S. racial
minorities and cultural minorities might say that this is a more accurate
and contemporary description of the American mind than the rest of us
would like to admit. And with Polk, racism joined with imperialism for
what was not the first nor last time in our history.

Our experience here in Mexico as we engage with indigenous civilizations parallels that of other North Americans who begin for the first
time to know a people and a culture that is not our own. We experience
a great awakening when the indigenous people we meet here invite us to
explore and evaluate our unconscious acceptance of Polk's "American
burden."

We meet intelligent people, not defective or underdeveloped North
Americans, people who love their children, are inventive and hard working. We meet people who know a great deal more about how to thrive in
their environment than we do. We become the "ignorant" ones among
them. We meet a people who are happy, and who wonder how we, as
a nation, could possibly do some of the things we do to other people in
the world, things we consider normal, rational, "justified." We come
to realize that these are people who, though they may be poor, are
not just playing the American game of competition, accumulation, and
consumption poorly. They are playing a different game all together.

This awakening experience is freeing and exciting. For suddenly, as
with the experience of the Grand Canyon, the world grows much bigger,
richer, more varied, and more full of possibilities than it was when we
defined ourselves and our way of seeing the world as the measure of its
possibilities and its grandeur.

This book invites you to join in an adventure that we hope will help
make the world bigger, richer, and more exciting for you as our privileged
life among the Mixtec peoples has done for us. We will visit villages that
have existed for thousands of years, meet their inhabitants, and talk with
them about life, economics, work, and family.

We believe that in our day the indigenous cultures of the Americas have things to say to our own culture, things that we need to hear. We hope the people you will meet in this book will communicate what they believe about the life of this planet to us all in a way that will help us reflect on our own hopes, dreams, and values.

Since most of us care about world poverty we are tempted to think that if only everyone in the world were to share the life standards of those in the United States, the world would be a much better place. But in our day this initial response has a serious flaw: the earth as a planet does not possess sufficient resources for all of the world's people to live as we currently do in the United States. In fact, according to the 2005 Ecological Footprint of Nations, published by Redefining Progress, we would need, astonishingly enough, nearly seven earths to provide the resources necessary for all of the world's inhabitants to share in the current U.S. lifestyle. The same report indicates that at existing global consumption patterns, we would "need 1.39 Earths to insure that future generations are at least as well off as we are now."[2] The world's people will *never* enjoy the lifestyle that people in the United States enjoy. Furthermore, we have *already* exceeded levels of consumption that can be sustained for the future, even if our population leveled out at current numbers.

The fact is we face two daunting challenges that no other generation has ever faced. First, the way of life and the economic articles of faith that emerged from Western European civilization require perpetual economic "growth," a growth that puts demands on the planet's resources and environment that it can no longer sustain. First World nations are driving the environment to changes which could make the planet unlivable for the human race.

But at the same time, economic growth itself requires the creation of "consumers" with "needs." We are successfully creating those consumers but with needs that cannot be met with our present economic and political systems and our current environmental position. As we create need, we create both perceived and real scarcity, an essential source of consumer demand. These real and artificial scarcities create our second great challenge, a gap between the extremely poor and the wealthy which has grown to dimensions that are socially unsupportable and will continue to lead us into political instability and war at levels that could dwarf the carnage of the last century of human life. These two challenges, taxing our environment beyond its limits and creating a socially unsustainable chasm between rich and poor, will force us to question and modify some of the most basic assumptions of our Western civilization if we are to survive the century.

And so we will first have to abandon Mr. Polk and the burden of America to be the hand of God on the planet. We will have to suspend the belief in the American Way of Life as a model for all the people of the globe and take the counter-intuitive leap of believing, for a few moments, that another culture may have something to teach us that we desperately need to know. We will need to seriously ask whether there is another game out there that is more appropriate to these challenges of our time.

If we are successful on this journey, we will not only learn something about how others see our culture, and something of the insights that their culture has given them. We will also see that the indigenous peoples of the world — the increasingly well organized poor of the world from small farmers' movements in India, to indigenous movements in Bolivia, and Zapatista guerrillas in Mexico — the ordinary people of the world are offering us a proposal for the future of this planet, a future without resource wars and without ecological disaster.

Could it be a more rational plan than the plan for ever expanding markets, ever greater consumption levels, and a globalization based on corporate control of resources?

We invite you to come with us to the Mixteca Alta of southern Mexico and decide for yourself.

Part I

Leaving Behind the U.S. Cultural and Moral Border

Chapter One

A Modest Re-Encounter
with Indigenous Communities
A Continuing Confrontation of Cultures

I walked up the steep, dusty road to the central village of the Mixteca
Alta, the indigenous area where I work in southern Mexico. Reaching the
top of the ridge on which the town stood I could see waves of hills, white
cut with the orange of deeply eroded slopes. Above was the ancient Black
Mountain, home of the center of the Mixtec civilization that thrived here
a thousand years ago. Tilantongo, as the village was once called, was the
ancient capital of the Mixtec kingdom of the indigenous Mixtec people
of Oaxaca, Mexico. Tilantongo reached its political and artistic peak
around 1000 C.E. Today it is called Santiago Tilantongo.

As I walked, I encountered two Mixtec women, their gray shawls
wrapped around their heads as protection against the sun, descending
from the village. We stopped to talk and I asked them why the town was
now called *Santiago* Tilantongo, after St. James the apostle.

"They say," one replied, "that the Spaniards stole the gold crown of
the king of Tilantongo long ago, and being a somewhat stubborn people,
we sent a delegation of Mixtec people to Spain to look for the crown.
The Mixtecs looked all over Spain but couldn't find it," she continued.

"But as they were preparing to leave to return to Tilantongo, they
went into a church, and there they saw a beautiful statue of Santiago.
So they stole the statue in exchange for the crown."

The statue still resides in the church of Santiago Tilantongo, as I was
able to verify, a church that sits upon the ruins of a Mixtec temple where
legends of miracles have grown up around it.

I told this story to a Mexican friend, a deacon who has spent his
life working with the indigenous people of this state of Oaxaca, where

The Church of Santiago Tilantongo

widely scattered villages house cultures with seventeen different languages and hundreds of dialects often unintelligible to neighbors in the next valley.

"There is a lot of symbolism in that story," was his reaction. Clearly, it says a lot about the original encounter of the Christian world of Europe with the indigenous world of southern Mexico. And that was one of my reasons for coming to what is called the Mixteca Alta, sixty miles northwest of the state capital city of Oaxaca, in the state of the same name.

When my wife and I first accepted work in southern Mexico as lay missioners with Maryknoll, a Catholic lay mission group working in poor areas around the world, I told a number of baffled friends that one of my hopes was to better understand the impact of Western European culture and its version of Christianity on the indigenous cultures of the Americas. I was frankly skeptical about claims that history had brought about a mutually beneficial blending of both Western and indigenous ways. What Mexican and Chicano friends in my adopted state of New Mexico had conveyed to me about the overpowering of their own culture, first by an aggressive, racist Anglo culture and again later by a well-meaning, liberal, college-educated population, added to my suspicions.

Forewarnings

I always feel a special presence each time I pass a spot on the sidewalk in front of the vacuum cleaner store on the main street in a small town in New Mexico, our home for twenty-one years before coming to Mexico. I'm tempted, each time I'm there, to walk around the spot, or, so as to not appear superstitious, just to inconspicuously cross myself. On that spot on the sidewalk my friend Greg Jaurequi died in 1992, bleeding to death from a gunshot fired by a homeless mental patient to whom he had many times given hospitality.

I ran into Greg shortly after our arrival in the small southern New Mexico town of Silver City, where we raised our children in the 1980s and 1990s. Over the years he and I worked together in the Mexican community on cultural and economic issues. Greg grew up in Silver City, went away to the university and then lured his young Anglo wife back to undertake a lifetime of defense of "his people," cut short by a bullet one summer night.

Greg grew up in the Chicano community in the 1950s and 1960s. In the 1960s he still experienced segregation like that between blacks and whites in the Deep South. The copper and zinc mines, where many of the men worked, enforced separate bathrooms and drinking fountains for whites and "Mexicans." A bitter strike broke out in the early 1950s when the Mexican American workers petitioned for equal wages and rights. Many of these "Mexicans" descended from the original inhabitants of that area before the United States forcibly took it from Mexico in 1848. The strike was brilliantly captured in 1954 by the film *Salt of the Earth* directed by Hollywood movie producers who were blacklisted for refusal to sign McCarthy era anti-communist oaths.

At the time we arrived in Silver City in 1979, *Salt of the Earth* was still too controversial to show openly. The Anglo culture that still decisively dominated the county politically and economically could not bear an open and honest portrayal of their oppression of the Chicano community. Greg remembered being thrown out of the "white" movie theater in town when he and a boyhood Anglo friend tried to attend together. The town landscape was clearly divided between Mexican and Anglo neighborhoods when we arrived in 1979, and fights frequently erupted between young people who dared to cross the racial boundaries.

Over the years we saw the open racism diminish, though having a foot in both worlds, we experienced the continuing racist feelings expressed at all-white gatherings.

By the time we left Silver City for Mexico in 2000, the open racism, which had intimidated Mexican parents into refusing to teach their children Spanish, had largely disappeared. Yet its economic and political consequences still remained. At that time, a new college-educated, artistic Anglo population began to arrive with little consciousness of the racial history of the area. This more progressive population offered a new solution to the cultural conflict of the area: "Let's forget it and work together like rational folks."

One segment of the Mexican community welcomed the invitation. Yet other sectors, either consciously or unconsciously (as in the case of the youth gangs) rejected the tempting outstretched hand. As I heard it expressed by a Filipino American friend, they seemed to feel that "until you recognize what you have done to my culture and people and learn to know me and my culture well enough to respect it for what it is, accepting your hand leads to cultural suicide for me, at the hands of your dominant culture."

We of the dominant culture underestimate the power of that dominance to wipe away the uniqueness of the other culture when we help others toward an equality that, in effect, offers them the option to "be like us." It doesn't often occur to us that people may not want to be "like us." Nor are we accustomed to asking whether it is in people's best interests to be like us.

Being the dominant culture, we come to think of ourselves as the norm and define other races and cultures in relation to ourselves. Ironically many of us white middle-class people may be only dimly aware of our own culture. Some years ago, the Catholic Diocese of Oakland, California, hosted a multicultural celebration. To the surprise of the organizers, the event attracted Latinos, Filipinos, Koreans, African Americans, and Vietnamese, but almost no white Anglos attended. The organizers surmised white Anglos perceived "culture" as something other people have. Cultural and racial dominance can make us blind toward our own cultural uniqueness and, more dangerously, can lead us to devalue other people's unique differences and histories.

Interestingly, it was not only Greg Jaurequi who gradually led me to understand this reality, but also friends from the small Afro-American Baptist church in our small New Mexico town. The local white Baptist church had long ago excluded these folks on racial grounds. Now, a new white generation was inviting their participation. Pat Ross and her preacher husband weren't sure about this offer. The black church had carried on a great tradition of Gospel singing and Gospel preaching as it exists only in Afro-American churches. In addition, their history had given them an understanding of U.S. society very different from that of most white Baptists. Did they really want all of this swallowed up by becoming a small minority in an "integrated" church?

So it was with all these uncertainties that I came to try to learn more of what it meant to be Mixtec in a *mestizo*-dominated and Catholic Mexico, and to see what this culture might have to teach us in the North.

Fiesta

On the December feast of Our Lady of Juquila, the most popular manifestation of the Blessed Virgin in the state of Oaxaca, my wife, Kathy, and I walked up the hills to the Church of San Javier in the Colonia of San Martín Mexicapan, where we lived, just on the outskirts of the state capital city of Oaxaca. By the time we arrived within three blocks of the church, the streets were almost impassable with crowds of people, booths of vendors selling *tacos* and huge crispy corn tortillas called *tlayudas* (see glossary), pirated CDs and DVDs, sweet breads, candies, candles, and rosaries. We slowly eased our way through the crowds, the music, and the bright lights toward the church, sampling some of the local foods on the way.

In the crush of the throng of the short, dark-skinned faithful waiting in front of the church to place their offerings of flowers or candles in front of the image of the Virgin, we were swept along by a force as strong as an ocean undertow. Being taller than the people in this throng, I could still look up through the trees and see the full moon looking down from the dark sky. I smiled to myself. I suspected the Universe was pleased with this silent and massive show of respect for the mystery of it all.

As the celebration continued into the night, they lit the "Castillo" (castle), an intricate thirty-foot tower of bamboo-like reeds and fireworks formed into myriad pinwheels and designs. In the night air the fire and explosions passed in miraculous sequence from one whirling pinwheel to the next climbing the tower toward an image of the Virgin outlined in flames. When the fire reached the Virgin's crown, it turned white hot, and the crown began to twirl slowly. Then, spinning madly, the white ring shot wildly upward toward the mutely waiting moon, and disappeared into the darkness amid the delighted screams of those who had come to pay homage. I laughed out loud, sure, now, that the Universe was indeed pleased.

I came to Mexico to learn more about the encounter between Western ways and indigenous ways. I already had many questions. And I learned that night that, yes, the indigenous people surely had accepted the faith that had invaded their land and in such an enthusiastic and profound form that it surprised me, and invited me to further explore and to understand more deeply the source of their celebration.

Out in the countryside of the Mixteca Alta I quickly learned that other pre-Hispanic rituals still were popular with some residents, although, as was the case in New Mexico, the people hid these rituals from the eyes of church representatives and white or mixed-blood *mestizo* people who were not known for their respect for other expressions of faith. I was told, numerous times, of unfortunate experiences that the indigenous community of the village of Apoala had had with a "gringo" family who lived there and desecrated some of the holy caves. Local people related how the resultant bad luck that fell upon the family led to the death of the wife and the sickness of the couple's son. This fate finally drove the family to leave Apoala, the spiritual center of the Mixtec people.

As I learned more about the life of this people, I found myself feeling a sense of relief that this unexpected encounter between religious traditions that began over five hundred years ago was not completely over. And I began to suspect that the indigenous spirituality, nearly annihilated so many years ago, still had things to teach us.

A Struggle Renewed

The encounter between the European and indigenous social systems also seemed to be continuing. An individualistic and acquisitive society, in 1514, met up with a communal society based on respect for family, community, and the natural world in these mountains of southern Mexico. And the struggle that began with that encounter, I was to decide, is still an open and spirited one.

Kathy and I have seven children. In late 1993 our oldest son, Chris, was traveling to El Salvador to visit his older sister who worked with war refugees there. A little after midnight on New Year's 1994, we came home from a party and turned on the blinking answering machine. "Hi, Mom and Dad. Happy New Year. I'm caught in a guerrilla war in southern Mexico, but I'm fine. Call you later."

It was Chris. But we "knew" that there was no war in southern Mexico. We were puzzled until, to our relief, he called back later that morning. He had been sitting on the plaza of San Cristóbal de las Casas, in the state of Chiapas that midnight when the rebel army of the EZLN, the Zapatistas, marched into town, scattering the astonished local police, who fled.

"Indigenous people came, many young kids, and some carried not guns but sticks carved to look like guns. They were very polite," Chris recounted. "And they handed out leaflets and gave speeches in the town square saying that they were in armed rebellion beginning this January 1, 1994, because it was the day the North American Free Trade Agreement (NAFTA) went into effect, and NAFTA meant death to the indigenous peoples of Mexico."

Indeed, this cultural struggle continued, and in fact it was just beginning to heat up.

Chapter Two

Cultural Genetics

Do We Need Cultural Diversity?

Biological Diversity and GM Crops

Perhaps it is not only true that we can, and indeed need to, learn from other cultures. It may also be true that a culture such as our "melting pot" culture loses the distinctive characteristics of the cultures from which it came and as it becomes more homogenous it develops a new vulnerability. We know that biological homogeneity breeds vulnerability. Could cultural homogeneity do the same?

Not long after we moved our family of six (and soon to be seven) children from Wisconsin to New Mexico in 1979, I became intrigued by a group in southern Arizona, the Native Plant Society,[1] which collects native plants and seeds. Members of the group recounted to us their experience of traversing the mountains of northern Mexico with horse and donkey in search of the ancient wild relatives of modern corn. Corn, they explained, was developed from the wild *teocintle* plant thousands of years ago. Now *teocintle* is threatened with extinction in some parts of Mexico.[2]

I learned from these people that when you reduce the varieties of any species of plant to just a few that closely resemble each other biologically, you put at risk the entire plant species. A single mutation of insect pest or plant disease that "discovers" that plant strain's weakness can devastate a homogeneous family of plants. However, when genetically diverse strains of the same plant family still exist, we retain the possibility of breeding in resistance to threatening new mutations.

In a nation like the United States, where monocropping large extensions of basic grains such as corn has become the model for "modern" agriculture, the genetic diversity of wild plant ancestors such as *teocintle*

Tilling the Fields in La Providencia Tilantongo

could play a key role in saving basic foods threatened by new disease or insect mutations.

My experiences in the region of Santiago Tilantongo have taught me much more about this topic.

There, I found Jesús and Fermina, campesino promoters from the Center for Integral Campesino Development of the Mixteca (Centro de Desarrollo Integral Campesino de la Mixteca, CEDICAM), where I am privileged to work. They were barefoot in the small field planting corn, black beans, squash, and amaranth. This mix of crops was typical of the true *milpa*[3] in which traditional indigenous campesinos plant complementary crops with great success. Jesús worked behind two young cow oxen, Morena and Blanca, opening furrows in the soft earth by pulling a hand-carved oak plow that resembles a one bladed chisel-plow. Behind him Fermina and their two children, Eduardo and Diana, nine and twelve years old respectively, followed, dropping seeds into the furrow and covering them with a quick, deft motion of their feet.

"When are you going to show me how to plow like that?" I yelled to Jesús as he and the ox team passed me.

"Now!" he replied, pulling the team to a halt. He explained to me how the oxen responded to voice commands and how to lean on the long wooden handle of the plow to adjust the direction of the furrow. If the furrow began to sag too far downhill, he would repeatedly call out the name of the downhill animal, *"Morena, Morena, Morena!"* and *Morena* would pull harder and straighten the plow.

I took off my shoes and took up the hand-hewn heavy wooden plow handle. But *Morena* and *Blanca* immediately sensed an ignorant hand and began to trot a crooked furrow across the hillside. I managed a couple of wavy lines back and forth across the *milpa,* while Eduardo and Diana laughed with delight. I handed the plow back to Jesús.

"That's enough for a first lesson," I conceded. "I'm wasting your time."

I turned to look at what Fermina, Diana, and Eduardo were planting. They each carried three distinct beautifully colored types of corn seed, a light whitish-yellow kernel, a brilliant mauve-red seed and a shiny blue-black variety.

"We plant all three varieties," Fermina explained. "That way, no matter what type of weather we have, one or the other will produce. For instance, if it is a very dry season, the white corn will not survive, but the blue and the red will do well."

"Every family in the village has varieties of corn that have been passed down in their family for generations," Jesús continued. "So in this one village we use dozens of distinct but related varieties of corn."

Indeed, across Mexico there are over fifty different "races" of corn that trace their ancestry to pre-Hispanic times. A recent scientific study suggested that the ancestors of Jesús and Fermina developed corn from the wild *teocintle* plant, whose seeds are smaller than a head of wheat, almost ten thousand years ago. Yet, indigenous scientists accomplished this feat, not by gradual experimentation but, it seems, in an astoundingly short period of one hundred years.

Jesús and Fermina and their Mixtec neighbors call the descendants of this miracle plant "criollo" corn. And they, as all Mesoamerican indigenous people, call themselves "people of corn." Considering that even today the corn tortilla makes up 47 percent of the calories of Mexican people, they literally are people of corn.

I was astonished to learn of the level of biological diversity represented in these corns. Hundreds of varieties of the major races still exist in isolated areas such as the Mixteca Alta, and they possess a wide variety

Passing native knowledge generation to generation

of characteristics that make them adapt and produce in all the climate regions and soils of southern Mexico.

In the Mixteca Alta, Jesús and Fermina and their neighbors use corn varieties that are still planted with the ancient *coa,* a long wooden stick with a shovel-like tool on one end and a sharp, metal-tipped, point on the other. They plant one such corn deep in the soil during the arid dry season and there it will grow up to four months without rain, an appropriate and ancient scientific response to unpredictable rainfall. Another corn has caught the attention of local researchers because it seems to have the ability to fix nitrogen from the air and into the soils where it grows.

Today, however, the campesinos are struggling against an invasive pest hardly dreamed of by the native seed gathering people I ran into in Arizona years ago. This new and dangerous pest threatens the incredible genetic diversity and utility that these plants, as well as the wild *teocintle,* preserve for our benefit. This pest is genetically modified corn.[4] Genes from the genetically modified varieties of corn produced by the

U.S. biotech giant Monsanto have appeared in traditional corn varieties, even though Mexico has not approved the planting of these laboratory-developed "freaks of nature." These patented genes pass from field to field through uncontrollable natural processes such as wind and insect movement, which seem capable of carrying pollen more than a kilometer from its place of origin and with unexpected rapidity can threaten to replace and eliminate important characteristics of invaluable pure varieties of traditional corn,[5] including its wild relatives.

If we consider the United States experience as a reliable predictor, where 85 percent of soy and cotton seed has been replaced with GM varieties, the invasion of genetically modified crops will damage and possibly destroy the capacity of indigenous communities of southern Mexico to carry on one of the most ancient and time-tested means of increasing biodiversity of domestic crops: the practice of saving seeds.

Already, 45 percent of all corn planted in the U.S. is genetically modified, and natural pollen drift from these crops has grown so widespread that U.S. corn farmers today save seeds only at great risk of being sued by Monsanto for saving and planting seeds containing its patented genes, which have inadvertently crossed with their traditional seed varieties.[6]

If indeed Monsanto succeeds in reducing the existing varieties of corn in the world to the few genetically modified varieties it markets, then it is possible that one single mutant disease could threaten the very existence of corn on the planet. And if at some point *teocintle* and the richly diverse corns of southern Mexico are eliminated, it is possible we will have nowhere to turn for genetic material that can serve as protection for our future corn sources.

Cultural Diversity and Healthy Human Beings

The practice of planting large areas of land with the same or similar crops can be called monocropping. If monocropping homogenous varieties of plants on a large scale can threaten to weaken biological species, what about monocropping human "monocultures"? The very idea of the North American "melting pot" seems to have been to smooth over the differences of migrants arriving from the various countries and cultures of the world and blend them into one homogenized "American" soup. This "soup" today more resembles a monoculture built around the activities of accumulating and consuming than it does a rich blend of the distinctive flavors of the participating cultural ingredients. Today, in spite of the statistical evidence that the standard cultural blend we have come up with and call the American Way of Life does not make us a happy people (look at our high rates of mental illness, drug use, suicide, and incarceration), we, through our television and films and through our businesses, market it to the rest of the world as the preferred way of life and the solution to life's basic challenges.

The human family is in the midst of perhaps the largest cultural experiment ever to be undertaken on the planet. The American cultural "blend," as portrayed in its movies, music, fast food chains, its transnational corporations, and its armies, promotes itself across the globe as no culture has ever before been able to do.

Cultural historian and ecologist Thomas Berry, in *The Dream of the Earth*,[7] sees the evolutionary process of the earth as "planetary self-education." The earth, a living organism including all human, plant, and animal life, is educating itself for the ends of the universe. "Human education," he continues, "can be defined as a process whereby the cultural coding is handed on from one generation to another in a manner somewhat parallel to the manner by which the genetic coding of any living being is communicated to succeeding generations." "This cultural coding is itself," he adds, "differentiated in a wide variety of patterns that characterize the various societies that are distributed over the planet."[8]

But today, one set of cultural coding (our own), like the genetically modified corn seeds, possesses the economic and military power to replace this wide variety of cultural patterns that exist in the world with one "monoculture." Could it be that cultural "monocultures," just as with biological species, are susceptible to mutant cultural diseases that such homogeneous cultures are unprepared to resist? As we reduce the variety of cultures in the world, are we putting the human family at risk? Will we be able to turn to the wide diversity of cultural wisdom of the human family to build in resistance to the cultural diseases, our violence, our psychoses, our suicide levels that put us at risk?

An authoritative study supported by The National Institute for Mental Health concluded that about half of Americans will meet the criteria for a DSM-IV disorder (mental illness) sometime in their life.[9] Is it possible that our small-in-population but globally dominant individualistic, aggressive, and consumer-oriented culture has already encountered the resistant cultural disease that it should most fear?

History is not lost in seeds. Native varieties of seed have immense biodiversity in themselves, a biodiversity gained through thousands of years of development "remembered" in the seeds' genetic bank. This diversity gives such seed great resistance to new threats. Could cultures also have such resistance in their memory bank? And do we eliminate this resistance as we eliminate this common memory?

If the culture of the American Way of Life succeeds in eliminating, for instance, the remaining indigenous cultures of the world, where will we turn for resistant cultural "genetic" material to heal and strengthen ourselves?

Mixtec Children on Culture

Sixteen families live in the village of San Isidro Tilantongo, and twelve children attend the tiny village school nestled between an expanse of white, barren mountainside and a patch of shady reforested alders where new soil is exploding into life with native grasses and wildflowers. My friend Jesús thought it would be interesting for the children to have a discussion with a North American, and he, too, wanted to hear what they would say upon meeting a culture from outside.

The seven- to twelve-year-old children wanted to talk about "cultural identity." As we approached the one-room school house, I could hear excited chatter and a commotion of desks and chairs being moved into place. Clearly, this was a special event for the children of this remote village.

Jesús introduced me, and I began asking them what it was like to be a Mixtec. What did it mean to be part of the Mixtec culture? Slowly at first, and then with growing confidence they began to describe their life, as I listed their answers on the chalk board.

"It's to speak our language," one girl suggested.

"It's about our music," a small boy added. "Like the 'Canción Mixteca.' "

Another girl thought for a moment and then said, "It's about respect. Respect for our ancestors and for other people."

"And respect for Mother Earth," another added.

"It's about working together doing *tequio* [the common work projects the villagers commit themselves to as part of their community obligations]."

I looked over at Jesús, who was beaming with delight, pleased with these responses. After we spent a full half-hour listing and discussing what it meant to be Mixtec, one boy raised his hand and asked, "Do you have a sense of cultural identity?"

I was caught off guard by the question. I had been concentrating on what the children felt about being Mixtec.

Taking a moment to collect my thoughts, I tried to explain that all of North Americans had ancestors and unique cultural roots, but that I, and most of us, had long since forgotten most of the elements of our original cultures. I struggled to try to explain to these seven- to twelve-year olds what was left over after these original cultural elements melted away. To say it's movies, or it's music, it's malls, or it's McDonald's all sounded so superficial after what the children had told me about Mixtec culture.

So what is it that we all share culturally in the U.S.? Democracy and advanced technology, of course. However, even though most of us U.S. citizens are unaware of it, from the perception of Latin Americans, some 500 million strong, we long ago lost our credentials as promoters of democracy. Even children in Mexico know much better than we do the history of decades of U.S. policymakers' interference in democratic processes in Chile, in Haiti, in Guatemala and the Dominican Republic, in Panama and Nicaragua — and in Mexico.[10]

Technology then? But I recalled that campesinos had told me about the new agricultural technologies that came with the so-called "green revolution" in the 1950s and 1960s and how this led to more concentration of land and wealth in the hands of the few here. Our U.S. culture now peddles genetically modified organisms.[11] "Was all of this so-called technological superiority anything more than a thinly veiled scheme for working with local elites to dominate other countries' economies and resources," I heard many Mexicans wonder. I had even heard one person express the opinion that the walk on the moon by U.S. astronauts was not real but had been staged to impress the world — such is the extent of the cynicism toward U.S. culture and political intentions.

There with the twelve children at the Mixtec school, I should have mentioned the democratic tradition of rebellion and solidarity of the great labor movements, the slave rebellions, the farmers' uprisings in New England, the Wobblies, the civil rights movement, the farmworkers' movement, the suffrage movement, and Chicano and Afro-American movements — all of this great struggle and dedication to freedom from the bottom up that forms our U.S. heritage. But it didn't come to me. That's not what I was seeing in us at this time in our history.

So I left it at that.

But I didn't have the last word. Before I left, another boy raised his hand and asked, "Do you really feel safe eating all of those big bloated grapes that are full of pesticides?"

Chapter Three

A Glimpse into the Mixtec World

Do These People Have Something to Teach Us?

The idea that another culture would have something deep and essential to teach us North Americans, something that we need to know for our well-being and survival, is counter-intuitive for most of us.

I was struck on a recent visit to the United States by some radio discussions on National Public Radio on the problem of eliminating poverty in a globalized world. For a while I couldn't figure out what bothered me about these well-intentioned discussions. Finally, I figured out that these discussions shared a troublesome presupposition that I had grown unaccustomed to hearing in Mexico, and in Latin America in general. All of these discussions seemed to begin with the assumption that we in the United States are the logical and principal source of the thinking and innovation that will solve global poverty. We are the ones who have something to teach the world.

The foundational assumptions on which such discussions rest have few contemporary counterparts among other cultures once we leave the U.S. borders and enter into the rest of the world. Ordinary people in many parts of the world do not see the United States as a part of the solution, much less as the one in charge of developing the answers to present-day crises.

This was brought home to me a couple of years ago when I was staying with a middle-class Mexican family in the city of Monterrey. Jesús Pacheco, then president of CEDICAM, and I were in the city for an international meeting sponsored by the United Nations on Financing for Development. A generous Mexican family hosted us for the three days we were there. Upon first walking into the family home, we noticed a small kitten limping across the front hallway to avoid our footsteps.

From an ancient codex of the only Americans with a thousand years of written history—the Mixtecs

Later, as we and the family were seated around the TV, the kitten jumped up in my lap. I asked the twelve-year-old girl, one of three children in the family, what had happened to the kitten.

"Our big, mean, dog bit it," she said, "and broke its leg! So now we keep it in here away from the dog."

"What's its name?" I asked, petting its small white-and-black spotted head.

There was an embarrassed silence in the room and the family members looked at one another rather sheepishly.

Finally the little girl spoke up.

"We thought you might be offended, but we call it...Taliban."

I assured the family that I wasn't offended and that I, too, was against the U.S. invasion of Afghanistan. The twelve-year-old's response was, "Well, everybody is!"

Once outside of U.S. borders the perception of who is the victim and who is the bully, who is part of the solution and who is part of the problem seems to do summersaults. Most of the discussions I have heard of problems of poverty or environmental challenges that occurred outside our border identify the U.S. as part of the problem rather than the so-lution. U.S. citizens may find this surprising, or even offensive. But it reflects a reality that we can ill afford to ignore or dismiss.

Could the different perspectives of the rich kaleidoscope of cultures that exist on this planet so brimming with life teach us something we need to know, something essential to a viable future for us and for the world? Could the Mixtec culture teach us something?

The Culture of Doña Soledad

On my first day with CEDICAM in the village of San Isidro Jalte-petongo on a barren mountainside of the Mixteca Alta I was with a group of campesino men and women from a neighboring village visiting a small project that produced medicinal herbs. I expected the Mixtec people to be reserved and quiet, as I had found many of the indigenous people of New Mexico to be. To my surprise, I was welcomed warmly in every home, each time with an alcoholic drink. In the first house I was served *pulque,* a mild drink made from the juice of the maguey plant. Subsequent households served *mescal,* a distilled liquor from the same plant somewhat similar to tequila. Toward the end they offered us store-bought beer.

When we sat down for lunch under a fruit tree, the hosts distributed flat, round, homemade breads, and the group of men and women switched the conversation from Mixtec to Spanish for my benefit.

"Wow, look how he speaks Spanish!" one of the men exclaimed.

"Where are you from?" another chimed in.

"The state of New Mexico, north of the border," I explained.

A chubby middle-aged woman, wearing the traditional brightly col-ored apron and gray shawl wrapped around her head against the sun, quickly joined in.

"Oh, take me with you there," Doña Soledad exclaimed.

The group erupted into loud laughter.

"It's not easy to get across the border," I parried, seeing myself getting pushed into a corner.

"Well then, take me with you here," Soledad replied.

The group broke into laughter once again. Evidently Soledad, as her name suggested, was indeed alone and husbandless.

"But I already have one woman," I tried to edge my way out of the direction the conversation was going.

"But why not two, don't you like Mixtec women?" someone replied, to more laughter.

Unable to extract myself easily, I let it pass, though from that day on whenever I arrived at Doña Soledad's village of La Unión Sayaltepec, I was greeted as her *novio,* or boyfriend.

The fun-loving nature of these people still impresses me. Only much later did Jesús admit that often in those first days he had been torn between his loyalty to his people and his friendship for me as they joked at my expense in Mixtec. It would, I mused, be worth my while getting to know these hospitable and fun-loving people.

Plowing with Don Agustín

Agustín León, a lean, vigorous, seventy-two-year-old campesino, welcomed me to his home in Tilantongo a short time ago.

"Felipito! I didn't know who it was driving up in that gray pickup. You must be a narco-trafficker. Who else could come in a different car each day," Agustín laughed.

"They stole my green pickup. So I have to borrow a different car every day from my friends," I replied, defending myself.

"Ay! Did they steal it here in Oaxaca?"

"No, in Cuernavaca."

"*Ven!* Come!" Agustín continued, excitedly. "Come and see my garlic that I planted, and the potatoes, too."

He dragged me up the hill through brilliant green plots of traditional corn, through a patch of peas, and on to where his garlic was just beginning to break the surface of the newly worked soil. We stumbled across a hand-carved wooden plow much like those the Spaniards introduced in the sixteenth century.

"I use that with the horses," Agustín explained. "I don't like to plow with the ox team. It's too slow. I used to plow with mules. They plow the fastest. But now I've slowed down to the horses. Seventy-two years old isn't just anything, you know. I think when I'm eighty-seven I may have to slow down and use the oxen."

Even after almost seventy years of farming, his enthusiasm for the land and his plants was contagious.

Agustín and the Mixtec people are a strong people who have, over the millennia, developed a way of life that they love. I recalled what I had often heard Jesús León say to assembled village campesinos.

"We're not campesinos because we are too ignorant to do anything else! We are campesinos because it is our vocation, an important vocation, one of the most important in the world since we all depend on food. And we have thousands of years of knowledge about the land that has been passed on to us as our heritage by our ancestors."

In time, I was to learn much more about Jesús and about this strong people.

Ancient Tombs

The small village of La Unión sits high on an eroded knoll in the mountains north of Oaxaca City. The U.N. estimates that the Mixteca Alta, where La Unión is located, lost an average of 5 meters of soil to erosion since the Spanish conquest. The whole village of La Unión was working on the barren hillsides at the gargantuan task of reforesting the white alkaline soil — that is, all of the village that was left. Only forty families live here now. They are the few that have been able to resist the poor soils, the lack of water, and the low prices they receive for their production since NAFTA (North American Free Trade Agreement) was signed in 1994. Over half of the village has had to migrate north to Mexico City or to the United States, where they work picking our vegetable crops or as waiters, dishwashers, and maids. They didn't want to leave but had to, to survive.

As we picked holes in the mountainside to plant the pine seedlings these few remaining villagers had carefully nurtured from local seed, someone yelled from below us.

"Come quick! Look at this!" one of the men had ceased digging and knelt on the white soil.

We all left our picks and shovels and hurried to where the man knelt. His shovel had uncovered a large, brown, flat rock, fully five feet in length and half as wide. Everyone seemed to know exactly what it was.

"Open it!" they exclaimed with excited but subdued voices.

Three men wedged their shovels under one side of the rock while others grabbed the rock's edge and swung it up like an opening door. As I watched the rock rise, I could see the carefully carved sides of what looked like a grave. The men rolled the rock aside, and we all stood gaping at the open tomb. The years had eroded brown soil into the opening. But small, brown-orange pieces of bone still stuck up from the loose soil.

Then, gently, talking in low voices, they began to sift through the loose dirt of the tomb and take out the obviously ancient bones. As they dug, they came across a round, white clay incensory, used perhaps in a funeral ceremony for burning incense, about a foot in diameter. How old was it? No one knew. Then they dug up some jade or onyx ax heads formed in the shape of a kernel of corn by the ancient indigenous civilizations that were this village's ancestors. Then someone pulled from the dirt a delicate, small, black vase, exquisitely made, no more that six inches high with a unique handle that, as we cleared the dirt from it, we saw also made a tiny spout for emptying the vessel.

Sifting through the rest of the dirt and finding no more relics, the dirt and the bones were carefully placed back in the tomb and covered once more and the ancient vessels were carefully set aside for display in the village community center. After a discussion about what should be done with the relics and the decision to save them in the village hall, we returned to our work, some no doubt musing about their own past and their ancient ancestors.

"Would that have been from before the flood or after the flood?" I heard someone ask the person working next to her. They were refer-ring to Noah and the biblical flood. And I realized to what extent this intelligent people, since the time of the European conquest, had been forced into ignorance even about their own history, perhaps especially about their own history. Indeed, part of the strategy of the conquering Spaniards was to eliminate the memory of a great and powerful civiliza-tion, including the written history in its books and codices, in order to assure continued submission.

The tiny, delicate vase continued to impress me with its unique design, and over the next few months, whenever I got to go to a museum of Mesoamerican history and archeology, I searched for anything similar in design. Finally, right near my Oaxaca City home, at Monte Albán, the well-known Oaxacan archeological site, I came across a vase quite similar, with its double-purpose handle and spout. The label dated it around 200 B.C.E.

From that time on I began to search out and pore over books about the Mixtec past. I began to think the people of La Unión could perhaps be excused for not being overly impressed when a North American culture that has existed for only two hundred some odd years informs them that it has the answer to the good life: that free trade and a growing economy and ever greater consumption patterns are part of the answer. And I began to discover that the Mixtec people have been living a good life in the isolated valleys of the Mixteca Alta for at least five thousand years.

In my reading I discovered that the Mixtec people are the only people in all of the Americas that has one thousand years of written history still in existence in their ancient codices — great, beautifully written and drawn books that tell their history from 600 to 1600 C.E. These beautiful books, which survived the Spanish and the Catholic Church's attempts to wipe out the original culture, evidently can be read as pictograms, ideograms, and also phonetically. They tell the stories of the great Mixtec kings and queens, priestesses and scholars, and also recount the cosmology and religious beliefs of this civilization.

The University of Leiden in Holland ranks the Mixtec civilization on a par with ancient Egyptian, Chinese, and Roman civilizations. Maartin Jansen, a well-known anthropologist from Leiden, writes: "One of our principal conclusions is that the Mixtec codices, in reality, contain great literature. They narrate dramatic histories on the level of the Greek or Shakespearean tragedies of Europe and are truly very profound."[1]

Compared to present times, women seemed to have enjoyed much higher status in pre-Hispanic Mixtec culture, which records famous queens, women scholars and scribes, as well as great women religious figures noticeably present in the codices.[2] However, this seemed to change with the arrival of the military men from Spain and the Catholic Church with its male priesthood professing celibacy. As I read, I began to look at the mountains and villages I passed each day in a different way, wondering what their significance would have been in a pre-conquest world. The Spanish arrived in the Mixteca Alta in 1519, and within thirty years of that date, the Mixtec population had been decimated.[3] Ninety percent of the Mixtec population were either killed or died of diseases. How many scribes, poets, sages, philosophers, scientists, and visionary leaders disappeared from the culture with those deaths, I wondered.

One day, as we passed the village of Sachio, built at the foot of a tall, pointed hill, I said to my friend, Jesús León, "You know what Sachio means, according to this book I'm reading?"

"No, what?" he replied with interest.

"It means "at the foot of the altar" or "at the foot of the platform.""

"Really?" Jesús replied. "How curious. That is very true to its name today. Every December 8 this little village is flooded with thousands of pilgrims who come for the feast of Our Lady of Juquila and walk up the mountain to the altar to ask or give thanks for favors from the Virgin!"

"And who knows what could really be underneath that curiously shaped hill where the altar sits!" I mused.

Shortly after that Jesús came up with a plan for a small portable library of books on Mixtec history, and CEDICAM began circulating the library through the scattered high mountain villages in a small portable bookcase.

Living History

But Mixtec history does not exist only in books and codices. To a remarkable degree it continues to thrive in indigenous social life and customs. More than once, urban Mexicans have told me the "crab joke" about Mexico and Mexicans. It goes like this:

> A North American was visiting with a Mexican friend, and as they walked through a Mexican marketplace they came to a stand where a woman was selling crabs. The woman had two barrels of crabs from which she selected what she was to sell. One barrel, which was covered with a close-fitting top, had the word "Japanese" written across it. The other barrel had no top. Across the front of this barrel was the label "Mexican." The Mexican man asked the woman why one barrel had a top on it, and the other had no top.
>
> "The barrel with Japanese crabs on it has to have a top on it," the woman explained, "or else the Japanese crabs will crawl out."
>
> "And the barrel without a top?" the Mexican man continued, looking quizzically at his North American friend.
>
> "Oh, they are Mexican crabs," she explained. "If one of them tries to get out, all the others will pull it back down."

Invariably, the point of this story for the urban folks recounting it is that it explains why Mexico and Mexicans never get ahead like North Americans.

In fact, this joke may represent a deep-seated fissure in the Mexican worldview that penetrates deeply into its indigenous past . . . and present.

Land in the Mixtec municipality of Santiago Tilantongo is held communally. This means that all of the land belongs not to individuals but to the community as a whole. The community allocates sections of land to families for crop production, and families pass these land parcels on to the succeeding generations. The community also maintains grazing and forest land available to all for grazing their sheep and goats and for cutting firewood. This communal system still exists to one degree or another in nearly all of the 570 municipalities, most of them rural, in the state of Oaxaca.

As the agronomist Angus Wright points out in *The Death of Ramón González*, the Mixtec worldview is based on the "image of the limited good."[4] In other words, we live in a reality where the good things of the earth are limited, where there is a fixed amount of good. For that reason, if one person accumulates a great deal of the world's wealth, that means someone else will be left with little or nothing. Life, according to the Mixtec people, in Wright's words, "is a zero sum game." Dominant U.S. culture prefers to think differently, and accumulation of personal wealth is seen as an appropriate goal. But as we will see, this Mixtec worldview leads to surprising consequences.

For instance, to this day, not only the landholding customs of Tilantongo, but many of its social customs as well, are designed to prevent the unjustifiable accumulation of goods.

My friend Fidel Cruz just finished a grueling three years of work as president of the commission of *bienes comunales,* communal lands, in Tilantongo. He carried out this work as a social responsibility, without pay, following the village's system of *cargos.* As in all of Oaxaca's indigenous cultures, the village expects each adult man, and now increasingly women also, to fulfill positions in the local indigenous governing systems a few times during his or her lifetime. To prepare for these unpaid positions, people need to accumulate enough resources to support the family during the period in which they will be taken away from their farming work. Most of a family's accumulation, then, is distributed back to the community in the form of unpaid service two or three times in a person's lifetime. This and other traditions such as *tequio* and *gueza* build into community life a stopping device or "brake" on excessive personal accumulation of the world's limited goods.

Tequio[5] is a system of community work projects to take care of community needs such as road repair or the construction of small school rooms. It obligates those who want to retain community rights to join in unpaid work in occasional community projects. *Gueza*, is a system of mutual giving that has been taken by Oaxacan tourists to be merely a great and beautiful dance festival celebrated each year in the capital city under the Zapotec name *guelaguetza*. In reality, both *guelaguetza* and *gueza* represent a voluntary but strict system of mutual giving, family to family, which further supports community life and discourages individual accumulation. In the dances done in front of tourists, communities give their art, dance, music, and poetry as a gift to the other communities present, and, on concluding the dances, throw gifts of the fruits or handicrafts typical of their villages to the spectators. Thus, what is one instance of a deep-seated and ancient system of mutual giving is mistaken for a dance.

In the Mixtec community *gueza* may mean that neighbor families help out with the costs of a wedding of a son or daughter, and the aid will be mutual when the neighbor families have a need. Or families will interchange work when the time for weeding fields comes, once the spring rains begin. Mixtec villages also appoint annual *mayordomos*. These individuals take responsibility for paying for all of the food, drink, and entertainment for specific village *fiestas*. Because of the economic burden, the community makes every effort to select members whose paid work has produced well. Those selected *mayordomos* consider themselves honored by their community. A young person would commonly aspire to one day be selected a *mayordomo*.

It is easy to see how people who have accepted a Western concept of "progress" and "development" might see these built-in leveling measures as backward, archaic, and anti-progress. Those who tell the crab joke no doubt have internalized such a Western concept of progress. In actuality, these leveling arrangements have supported fulfilling and viable lifestyles among indigenous communities for thousands of years. The viability of the Western notion of "progress" and its ability to sustain human communities for more than a few hundred years, in contrast, has yet to be tested.

In the United States, we prefer to view the distribution of the world's goods not as a zero sum game but as one in which the overall "pie" regularly increases in size due to technological and economic growth and innovation. Using this assumption, if an individual's work makes the pie grow substantially, then this person can legitimately be expected to claim a larger slice of the pie. When the whole pie, or the whole economy, increases in size, then everyone's slice of the pie increases. This economic worldview based on the assumption of an "unlimited good" gives legitimacy to the accumulation of individual possessions, even to the extreme, because it assumes that this will also ensure that the needs of all are simultaneously being met.

Yet we live in a twenty-first-century world where the ecological limits of the planet are now clearly evident, and where every year more millions of the world's populations are refused even a small taste of the pie. It would seem obvious that this assumption of an infinitely expandable base of wealth needs to be reexamined.

One could say that Mixtec society and U.S. society are playing two very different games with the way they organize their social and economic lives. Moves that are appropriate in one game, say unlimited accumulation of goods and wealth in the United States, may be inappropriate in the other, the Mixtec game. What is the right game to be playing for this twenty-first century?

Privatizing Land, Privatizing Culture

The Mixtec indigenous communal culture is under attack here in Mexico. Government programs are pushing a privatization that threatens to once again concentrate lands in the hands of Mexican and foreign elites, much as was the case before the Mexican Revolution of 1910. Virtually all Mexican banks are now foreign-owned, and nationally owned industry has diminished drastically, while changes in the Mexican constitution under pressure from NAFTA have allowed agricultural and communal land to be sold to foreign entities.

Recently I joined in with Jesús León and Fermina Zarate's neighbors, weeding the lush field of black beans that they had planted in their village of San Isidro Tilantongo and fertilized with the castings of thousands of red worms. The plants were bigger and with a deeper green than the nearby beans of a neighbor who had used chemical fertilizers. (So were the weeds.)

This common work we were doing was a *gueza,* one of the many forms of mutual giving mentioned above. Neighbors would give their labor, and Jesús and Fermina would do the same for the neighbors. The day was special, as we sat down in the grass at the edge of the field for a lunch of black beans, tortillas, and raw *chiles.* The late summer air was fresh and cool, and the sky blue with wispy white clouds. Loma Larga, or Long Hilltop, as this field was called, was thick with stands of native corn, beans, and squash. In the distance, Monte Negro (Black Mountain), the home of ancient Mixtec communities and one of the largest mainly unexplored archeological sites in this part of Mexico, stretched to meet the sky.

I told the group that I had met some engineers from the government geographic offices when I had driven into the community. They were working for PROCEDE, a federal government project to determine the legal boundaries of community and family parcels.

"They won't come here!" Jesús responded forcefully.

I understood Jesús's strong feelings better a few days later when I attended a national meeting of campesinos concerned about possible privatization of water resources in Mexico and heard people from communities around the country describe how the privatization process concealed within the government PROCEDE program was dividing villages, provoking increasing violence, and causing communal lands to end up in the hands of people from outside the villages. At the same meeting a University of Mexico professor from Mexico City, Andrés Barreda, explained his understanding of the goals of current Mexican government policy. "The goal is to reduce the campesino population of the Mexican countryside from 25 million to 1 million. That way the mineral, water, and forest resources can be exploited with foreign investment without interference from the rural indigenous peoples."

Back on the Loma Larga, Jesús explained. "We're some of the few who are refusing these programs. We are more traditional in many ways. Sometimes they call us 'Indians' and think we are backward. But we'll always have our lands."

Ancient Rules

The Mixtec people are different from us not only in their understanding of economics and ownership.

A while back I came across an ancient Mixtec poem that was recited when new authorities took over their *cargos,* or traditional governing responsibilities, each year in the village of Santiago Apoala. It struck me as being an impressive combination of idealism and realism, as it counseled the new authorities on their responsibilities to the community. Perhaps it represented a wisdom that was part of what had made these communities survive for thousands of years. With the highly valued poetic sense of the Mixtec, the outgoing authorities each year recite:

> With great care and veneration
> We all come together
> For the consecration
> Of our authorities.
>
> For this purpose this day is set aside
> In which our authorities begin
> With the full weight of responsibility
> With the "cargo" of the people.

Whether going uphill
Or whether going downhill
This way and that way
All for the welfare of the community.

For to be so employed
Is nothing but problems
Our authorities do many tasks at once
Two or three at the same time.

So may you pardon and bear with us
May you stay firm for your people
May you bear it for us all
Like this flower that we place in your hands.

May your heart be made strong
Strong like this flower
That lives among the rocks and cliffs
And grows in the wild winds.

So that this way no brother will suffer
No citizen, poor one, or orphan
So that no harm will be done to our villages, neighbors,
We wish all peace and tranquility.[6]

The day after I read it I took the poem with me and showed it to Alfonso López, a CEDICAM campesino promoter from the village of San Pedro Cántaros, near Santiago Apoala, the town that is the legendary center of origin of the Mixtec people in their creation narrative.

"Alfonso, you've got to see this!" I began.

He stopped and looked questioningly at me.

"This poem, look, do they still use this in your village when they are changing authorities?"

He took the book from me and turned through the pages.

"Sure," he said, surprised at my amazement. "But in Mixtec."

Poetic rules for a very ancient and a very different game.

Part II

Ancient Alien Values

Chapter Four

A Mixtec Teaching about Work

Work, Tequio, *and a Day at the Office*

A few months ago I enjoyed an unusual opportunity to get a different perspective on some important aspects of my life: work, celebration, and community. I attended a festival celebrating corn and its place in indigenous life and communities. Indigenous people here, as we have seen, call themselves "people of corn," and throughout the course of ten thousand years they have developed dozens of races and hundreds of varieties of native corn from the wild plant called *teocintle.*

A group of Mixtec campesinos at the festival recently demonstrated how they worked together when it was time to harvest the corn. As they acted out the ritual still used in their communities, first the family whose plot was to be harvested went to friends and neighbors and asked them to join in to pick their harvest. This expresses *gueza* in Mixtec communities and involves the commitment to return the favor. Everyone agreed upon a date, and that morning all showed up with family members and burros to take the corn from the field to the family home.

The many hands harvested ears of corn from the field and created a mountain of corn on a designated area on the edge of the family plot. There the owners of the harvest made a simple cross from the stalk of the best corn plant found, and hung the two best ears of corn on the cross before implanting the entire cross on the top of the mound. The owners then secretly hid a bottle of *mescal* (distilled liquor made from the maguey plant) in the mound and poured on top a few drops of the blood of the turkey that had been killed for the community meal that would follow in a symbolic offering back to Mother Earth in thanks for the bounty received. The helper who first found the *mescal* as he loaded his burro from the pile of corn ears became the *mayordomo* of

A tequio, *or community work project, building a greenhouse in Zaragoza,* *Tilantongo*

the *mescal* with the honor of serving the drink to all during the day and also of being the recipient of the two best ears of corn hung on the cross to save as seed for his next year's crop.

After all the trips by burro to the family home had been completed and the corn stored away, all sat down to a meal of turkey and *mole* (a famous, Oaxacan sauce, pronounced MO-lay, and made of almost thirty ingredients including chocolate, peanuts, and *chile*). The first plate of food was turned over on the ground under a small altar on which a candle burned, as a small return to Mother Earth for her generous gift of corn.

"Not like your typical day at the office," I mused. Was this what work could be like? What had I and my culture done to strip away from work its celebration, its community, its ritual? Were we really the better for what we have made of work: something that has to be done before we can get to the fun stuff? Work in the United States seldom has these rituals or traditional celebrations to go with it. And clearly, personal accumulation of wealth was not the primary purpose of this kind of work. Are these ancient understandings of work completely alien to our North American world, or do they have something to teach us? What could we learn from this, and how could we apply it to our own work?"

Work in the Land of Quetzalcóatl

Perhaps the Mixtec people have it right. Perhaps our work has more significance than a necessary chore that provides for our needs and our consumer desires. Perhaps it should also be a celebration. Perhaps it also has an importance in the great scheme of things that we underestimate.

Physicists and cosmologists today tell us we are part of a growing universe still in the process of self- (or divine) creation. As the only known conscious and reflective species in this universe, perhaps we have a special part to play in this universal creative process. Could it be that human work, whether paid or unpaid, forms an integral part of this creative process? Thomas Berry in his book *The Great Work* (1999) suggests, for instance, that "The Great Work now, as we move into a new millennium, is to carry out a transition from a period of human devastation of the Earth to a period when humans would be present to the planet in a mutually beneficial manner."[1]

Archaeologist Laurette Séjourné, in *El universo de Quetzalcóatl* 1994, points out that in the worldview of the Mixtecs' ancient ancestors, the place of human effort, human work, was to transform the mundane into something more closely representing the divine. This spiritual concept of the importance of human work inspired a whole civilization to creative effort that transformed the Mesoamerican jungles into one of the richest centers of human art in the world of its day.[2] The work of the ancient Mayans at Tikal in Guatemala, and Copán, in Honduras, as well as the work of the Mixtecs and Zapotecs at Monte Albán and Mitla in Mexico, among many others, give testimony to this creative surge.

Séjourné's participation in first-hand archaeological digs reveals a fascinating aspect to the civilization that created the great pyramids and art of Mesoamerica. The product of this inspired human work — buildings, frescoes, pottery, etc. — was ritually destroyed every fifty-two years, the length of the indigenous "century." Séjourné sees this as an intentional statement that for these ancient indigenous peoples, the point of work was creating, not possessing: "This interior detachment or freedom in the face of these superb objects leads us logically to the conclusion that the importance rendered to such works did not reside in the thing itself, as in our materialistic societies, but in the process of creation, in the impulse that converts inert matter into ideal forms."[3]

There is the story of a Mexican vendor who was approached by an American tourist. The tourist, impressed by the finely worked small weavings the woman was selling, decided to buy them all.

"How much would it cost me to buy all that you have?" he asked, thinking of how friends would appreciate them as gifts and how he could resell the rest for a good profit.

"Oh, I couldn't do that," the vendor replied without hesitation.

"But why not?" the astonished tourist stammered back.

"Because then I would have nothing to sell," the woman earnestly explained.

I have heard variations of this story. If it did not actually happen, it is still very believable in a Mexican context. I have heard it both from those who thought the vendor was foolish, and from those who saw that here were two very different concepts and cultures of work failing to communicate with each other. To the vendor, the selling activities, chatting with friends, receiving old customers, dickering over prices with new customers, watching passersby, was equally as important as the profits made at the end of the day. For the tourist, the only rational point to the day's work was the money gained.

I have had the privilege of doing many kinds of work in my life. Although I spent many years in school, my only expertise is in not being an expert. I have worked in construction, as a bus driver, a janitor, and a small farmer. I have worked in steel factories, done cleanup in egg processing plants, kept bees, been a ranch hand, sold seed, taught high school, sold vegetables, and helped start cooperative businesses. I've taught philosophy, taught English, fixed toilets, repaired roofs, and worked on city paving crews. In most of these jobs I have run across the occasional person who knew how to make the work day into a creative process instead of a necessary chore. These were generally the happiest people I would run into. They, like the Mixtec farmers, knew how to see the challenge in finding creative ways to do their work or in finding creative ways to enjoy the human beings with whom they worked. They seemed to understand their work as a creative calling, a vocation, rather than a job. Interestingly, some of the most creative workers I've known, in the United States as well as in Mexico, have been small farmers.

These decades of work have taught me that we regularly make technological, political, and economic choices that increasingly undermine our ability to value work as a creative task. First, we have allowed technological choices made by others and technological products themselves to shape our work life, the pace at which we live, and our self-image as workers. Second, we have permitted the politics of a corporation-centered version of democracy to remold and devalue our human work.

Finally, we have allowed the promoters of "the mall culture" to redefine us as consuming creatures rather than as creative workers.

Hay Bale Technology

While our families were trying to make a living off organic farming on the grounds of a Franciscan monastery in the mid-1970s, my friend Virgil and I used to hire ourselves out to neighboring farmers putting up hay to bring in a few extra dollars. The days were hot, and the dust from the baler we rode behind filled our noses and covered our clothes. We were always glad when lunch break came, and we could sprawl for a few minutes in the shade of the half-filled hay wagon to eat a sandwich. One day the old farmer for whom we worked and who had run the tractor all morning, lounged back in the shade next to us and unwrapped his own sandwich. Soon, he turned pensive and said, "You know, it's odd. Years ago before we had these balers, we used to put up hay like this. But when it came time for dinner at mid-day, we would stop work, walk into the farm house, and eat a hot meal of meat and potatoes and then walk back out to the field for the rest of the afternoon. And we always got all our work done. Why is it that now with all these new machines, we don't have time to do anything but grab a quick sandwich?"

That, of course, got me thinking about who decides what technology we will use. How do we decide what purpose we really want the technology to serve? Do we often ask whether the particular technology that we use really makes life better for us?

The point was brought home graphically and tragically the following spring when this same farmer's adult son was planting corn. The son hurriedly finished planting all the corn acreage and was on his way to the cow barn to begin milking, when he suddenly noticed he had broken a hydraulic hose on the planter. This meant the planter speed would have been wrong all day. He had planted the expensive seed too far apart, and the hundreds of acres of feed corn would never be able to be cultivated correctly. He worried that it might not even pollinate well enough to produce the corn ears.

When his parents arrived home, they found a note on the kitchen table. They found their son's body next to the family shotgun in the hay loft of the barn. Is it partly the technology we have "chosen" that forces us to work under such pressure that we put ourselves in these untenable situations?

Later, we heard of a monastery farm in Indiana where they had bought such big planting equipment that in order to make it pay, they had to put up lights in their fields and work far into the night to keep up with the planter. Who really makes these technological choices in our society? And what is the purpose these technology creators have in mind? How much do these choices change the quality and the style of our lives?

In the late 1960s and early 1970s, at the dawn of the cybernetic age, there was much talk in the media about how the new technology was going to speed up our work so much that we would have a four-day work week and longer regular vacations. The challenge of the future, the pundits announced, would be how to creatively use all the free time computer technology would provide us. School counselors advised high schoolers to develop new hobbies and interests, because there would be so much more leisure time. But someone hijacked that dream along the way. Because computers make it possible to produce more work faster, more work per day is expected. Computer technology, for most of us, has translated into higher expectations and more work, not less. How many of us stop to eat a leisurely evening meal with the family today? How many of us work evenings and weekends? And who has this "time saving technology" really served? Only the few high tech billionaires and millionaires who were able to reap big profits from the high tech explosion of the 1980s and 1990s?

The campesino farmers of the Mixteca have experimented with technologies. They have tried miracle seeds and green revolution technologies and have found them inadequate for their life goals. They have sifted other technological options, new and old, tractors and chemical fertilizers, animal power and ancient native seeds, and chosen what serves their lives. Are we intelligent enough to do the same? Or are we content to have technologies someone else says we need dictate how we live?

As we see the difference between what work means in the Mixtec society, and in our Western technology-based society, I suggest that we begin to think about which kinds of technologies serve life, which technologies make life more beautiful, more satisfying, healthier, and more sustainable. Do we still have the space within our society to say "no" to technologies that do not serve these very basic purposes? Perhaps we must first learn to outgrow the deeply imbedded prejudice that technology will solve the world's problems and provide us a happy life. If we, like the Mixtecs, can select technologies according to their usefulness to our life goals, instead of leaving the choice to those who develop and promote a technology, we will cease to allow technologies to determine the nature and value of our work. Only then will we be able to intelligently use technology instead of being used by it.

Does this mean giving up the cell phone or iPods? What we will choose to give up and to keep, to accept and reject for the future will be based on a basic change in the way we look at technology and in the way we evaluate it. This change in attitude might require us to be willing to change game plans, if not the game itself.

Labor in Today's Market-Driven, Corporation-Driven Economy

Though we, as a nation, tend to disparage the value of physical work, I have often found what we call "manual labor" creative and fulfilling. Certainly the work of the Mixtec corn harvest was both — not only for the indigenous people. Most of us would also agree that what they described would seem inventive and satisfying work.

Today, it seems, a lack of attention to the value and dignity of work in the U.S. culture renders us complacent about the vast erosion of the importance of labor, of adequate working conditions and the just compensation that workers once possessed. This erosion is not accidental, but the chosen path of a political and economic model determined to extract maximum profit at the direct expense of the worker. This is not the consequence of actions of "mean individuals" in management so much as a systemic direction of our economic model. With a few notable exceptions, corporate executives appear as impotent to alter the economic model as are the workers. The problem lies in how our corporate economy actually works, its logic. No rational, thoughtful person or group sits "at the controls" asking the Mixtec question about what serves our life goals. Instead, the CEO and board of directors focus on profit, expansion, and earnings for the stockholders.

A while back I read comments by an advisor to Kofi Anan[4] suggesting that the poor working conditions and continuing poverty in "developing" countries need to be seen in the context of history. That is, U.S. and European workers occupied an analogous position a century ago and the situation of workers in the poor countries merely means that they lag behind on the road that eventually led to improved worker rights in the developed Western economies.

People who talk this way don't seem to know much about U.S. labor history. The advantages that workers have in the United States, at least those left after the last thirty-five years of policies that have dismantled labor laws and rolled back anti-trust legislation, did not arise spontaneously as a natural product of the path of Western development. These advances, these just wages and working conditions, were violently resisted by the corporate elite of their day. Workers' rights in the West were won with many deaths in the streets and factories of European and American economies, by hangings like those of the Haymarket martyrs[5] and by desperate organized labor struggles. They are not the inevitable result of the advance of Western economic development.

Furthermore, they were gained only by forcing government to take a strong role in controlling corporations and aiding in redistributing wealth. Why would we believe that progress for laborers will occur today in "developing" countries without the same tragic sacrifice by workers in the streets and factories of the world? Unfortunately, improvement in workers rights will be much more difficult today because of the immense power that unregulated transnational corporations have acquired to create and implement labor policy around the world to suit narrow and purely corporate interests. As if this is not enough, as the "liberal" economic model eliminates strong government from more and more areas of our lives, workers lose the one ally essential to achieving what progress they have made over the years. The reality is not so much that we are at different places on the same road. We are on the wrong road for any kind of social progress and equity for workers in the future.

All this is true not only for the workers in developing countries. The current model of trade liberalization and corporate globalization pits workers against one another across the globe to achieve the greatest output at the lowest possible level of wages and benefits. A "flexible labor force" both at home and abroad allows large corporations to function without interference from unions, employing people at schedules that avoid obligations to provide benefit packages, and at wages that leave some full-time workers employed below the poverty level. In this way, Wal-Mart in the United States externalizes the true cost of its labor force onto the rest of us U.S. taxpayers, since many of its employees earn wages below the poverty level and are forced to turn to tax-supported government programs, like government food stamps, to survive. A report by the minority staff of the U.S. House of Representatives Education and the Workforce Committee projects that one two-hundred-person Wal-Mart store costs federal tax payers $420,750 each and every year in federal benefits paid to Wal-Mart's workers.[6] Wal-Mart operates over a thousand stores in the United States.

At the same time that it denigrates the dignity of our human work, contemporary corporate evolution not only eats up scarce government tax funds by externalizing the real costs of corporate operations onto government poverty programs. It also eats up local community capital by diverting the circulation of dollars to shareholders and executives residing outside the community. According to a study done in 2003 by the Institute for Local Self-Reliance, of every $100 spent at a locally owned enterprise in Mid-Coast Maine, $45 returns to the community. Of the same $100 spent at a national or international chain, only $14 remains in the community to strengthen its local economy. A similar study carried out in Austin, Texas, yielded nearly identical results.[7]

"Market forces" determine our lives. We, who see ourselves as the most powerful and advanced nation on earth, have abandoned ourselves, our children, our grandchildren, and our earth to what we call "market forces"! Unfortunately, except for perhaps the top 5 percent of the U.S. population[8] it's not working, not even in the United States, let alone for the half of the world that earns less than $2 per day.[9]

The Vocation to Consume

In an era of Wal-Marts, shopping centers, and TV advertising, we are allowing ourselves and our very concept of human nature to be recast by a dominant commercial sector of our society. We are literally being re-visioned, not as creative workers, participating in the evolving universe, or the indigenous artisans giving form to the Mesoamerican jungles, but as passive and easily manipulated consumers. From all sides we are bombarded with specious propaganda that portrays the purpose of human life as ever greater levels of consumption.[10] Most of us get a full tree's worth of junk mail in our mailbox each year.[11] Individual stores mail advertisements, mail-order companies send catalogs, television and billboards hype products. Shopping malls have become our cultural centers. Parents allow teens to spend entire Saturdays at the malls, shopping and "hanging out" with friends, where they can't help but be exposed to the latest teen clothing fads. The ultimate degradation and shame to which an individual can arrive is poverty — generally, in the United States, not a poverty that means hunger, though that also exists, but a poverty defined as the inability to purchase and consume as many others do.

President Franklin D. Roosevelt, with some success, reigned in the Wal-Marts of his day, restraining the unbridled "market forces" that led to the Great Depression. Much of the successful legislation that he helped to create has been dismantled since the 1970s in order to provide substantial benefits to the large corporate sector of our economy.[12] But Roosevelt's caution becomes even more relevant for us today than in the 1930s when he counseled us that "happiness lies not in the mere possession of money" but rather "in the joy of achievement, in the thrill of creative effort."

Yet what work means for us and what kind of work we will have, in our future, will depend on what economic game we choose to play, with what goals and by what rules.

Creative Work

In the early 1980s, in the most eroded and impoverished lands of southern Mexico, three young Mixtec campesinos along with two indigenous farmers from Guatemala who had recently escaped the U.S.-supported massacres of indigenous villages by the Guatemalan government,[13] looked across a desolate landscape in Santiago Tilantongo, Oaxaca. Against all reason and decades of local resignation, they envisioned a lush future for these barren mountainsides. And they formed a campesino-based organization, the Center for Integral Campesino Development of the Mixteca (CEDICAM), to help build that future.

Reviving an ancient technology of hand-dug contour ditches, they began to cover hillsides with the curving bands of one meter deep trenches. When the rains came driving down in the coming summers, the soils that were once eroding down the hillsides in deep brown gushing torrents now were retained by the contours of the terraces. The soils below the ditches retained more moisture, and crops began to improve. Neighbors saw the results and began to join in community work projects to extend these ditches to more hillsides.

But when these visionary young men began to plant trees in areas where communal pasturing of goats was common, the villagers ridiculed them. "Why do you want to plant trees?" they laughed. "You can't eat them."

But the visionaries were not to be diverted from their goals. They experimented with tree seedlings from the government and found them inadequate for the climate of the area. They began their own tree nurseries, collecting seeds from the few remaining native trees. Little by little they successfully urged the village shepherds to keep their goats out of areas where the new seedlings struggled to put down roots. Careful observation taught them that the large, fertilizer-fed seedlings of the government didn't "take hold" in the dry, alkaline soil. But their small, naturally fertilized trees spread their small root systems and began to grow, green and promising in the weak, semi-arid soils.

In a few years, the once barren hillsides shone light green with thousands of native seedlings. They experimented with new local varieties, transferring seedlings from trees that were thought to only grow in the riverbeds, to the adjoining hillsides and discovered that the *elite,* a leguminous species of alder, grew quickly on the newly terraced slopes. Its leguminous leaves decomposed quickly creating new soils under shade not seen on these hillsides for generations.

In a few years the villagers no longer needed to walk miles to collect firewood for cooking their beans and tortillas. They gathered all the wood they needed simply by pruning the new young forests that were beginning to cover the nearby hillsides.

Today deep forests grow where once the young campesinos looked over barren *arroyos.* The contour ditches are not only holding soils in place but are also recharging the aquifers below the mountainsides, and in turn, the springs on which the villages depend for water run more freely. In the last five years, villagers of Santiago Tilantongo have planted over 1 million new native seedlings. A land and a culture are being reborn.

This is work at its most creative and its most human level, where human beings are not passive consumers but intelligent participants in our universe's creative momentum. How could we make such work a part of our future?

Chapter Five

Money, Wealth, and Mixtec Fiestas

Which Cultures Create Wealth and Which Create Scarcity?

But it is not only our ideas about work that we need to examine in the light of some values that may seem alien to us. Our concepts of wealth and money could also use some re-evaluation.

As Kathy, our youngest son, Dominic, and I were driving along a dirt road last summer, approaching a remote indigenous village in the Mixteca Alta, where we had been invited to attend a fiesta, we crossed paths with our friend "Chucho" Jesús Pacheco. He was driving the village's old communal pickup truck on his way to Nochixtlán to pick up the *cohetero* who would assemble the *castillo* and other fireworks for the fiesta. *Coheteros* make a good living hand-making all the fireworks and designing all the fireworks displays for village celebrations.

"The fiesta is just beginning...I'll be back soon," he waved us on toward his village of Tierra Colorada (Red Earth) Apoala. A few minutes later we emerged out of the woods overlooking the village. Below, amid a cluster of rough-hewn, windowless, log cabins with a mixture of pointed thatched and tin roofs, a huge circus tent rose above the center square of the town of 168 souls. To one side the small spires of the new community chapel ascended, all built by *tequios,* donated community work. The chapel was going to be dedicated in this weekend of fiesta.

In spite of the June heat wave sweeping the rest of the state of Oaxaca, the evening air was cool in this high mountain village. We parked our car — one of the few in the entire village — behind the new chapel, and walked through the crowds toward the huge yellow and green striped tent, where large tables with tablecloths had been set up. Two gracious young village women greeted us and, after a few giggles at the unexpected

Community production of vegetables in San Antonio, Tilantongo

appearance of three tall "gringos," pinned finely worked tiny souvenir woven hats and baskets on our lapels as signs of welcome. These palm souvenirs symbolized the ancient craft of basket weaving practiced in the village from pre-Hispanic times. The town was hosting a palm weaving contest on the next day where weavers would demonstrate their skills. Our hosts sat us down and served us a rich meal of finely flavored mutton and vegetables with large tortillas homemade from traditional native corn. The hosts also offered soda, beer, and *tepache,* a lightly fermented local drink of pineapple and sugar cane, to a campesino crowd of hundreds under the bright tent. A barefoot old campesino man with grizzled white beard and well-worn clothes sat down next to us. It was difficult to surmise his age.

"What would you like to eat first?" our hostess asked him.

"To the stomach of a poor man, everything tastes good," he replied with a toothless smile, as he began with a bowl of mutton stew. Miguel, a friend from a neighboring village who happened to be playing in the band for the dance that night, caught my eye from across the huge tent, and came rushing over to talk.

"Yeah," Miguel explained to us, "here in Tierra Colorada Apoala they've invited all the villages that share boundaries with them, and they're committed to give food and drink free to whoever comes for two days straight." Food kept arriving in abundance in the hands of the long-skirted young women. I thought about what this tradition reveals about indigenous values regarding the accumulation of wealth. On a village or on an individual level, accumulation of wealth does not constitute a value in itself nor does it function as a tangible sign of one's success in this game of life. Rather these indigenous people accumulate wealth so that it can be given back to the community in fiesta, in celebration of and gratitude for life.

In the growing darkness we soon processed in *calenda,* the name for the ever present parades that accompany fiestas, to the sound of a brass band across newly plowed fields to the house of the *madrina* — the woman who had underwritten the cost of the parade and the giant dancing mardi gras–type puppets that joined in our procession. Inside each huge papier-mâché puppet a young man or woman danced the traditional area dances, with the puppets' skirts and arms spinning in wild, rhythmic cadences. Then, we processed to the dark wooden hut of the *mayordomo* of the candles, who sponsored thirty large white candles used in the dedication Mass. As we approached the dark cluster of cabins where the *mayordomo* lived, to one side of the path a half dozen men and women worked in the shadows over large wooden vats of blood and bones, butchering a cow to feed the multitudes for the next day's meals.

"What an abundance of food this tiny valley produces!" I found myself thinking. And then I began musing on the paradoxes of food production and hunger that we were learning about from these Mexican campesinos.

What causes hunger in poor Mexican communities and around the world I wondered, and what are the solutions? It seems that Tierra Colorada, using teams of oxen, native seeds, green manures, and organic methods both new and old is able to feed itself in abundance. But what has happened to cause this to change for many other villages and for many rural Mexicans? For rural poverty in Mexico hovers between 70 percent and 80 percent and hunger is on the increase.

Wealth and Money

As I thought about it further, I reflected that hunger and poverty in Mexican villages and around the world seem to arise from some specific types of scarcity — often directly generated by the current economic system itself.

But here, we need to first make a distinction between "wealth" and "money" in order to clearly perceive how a system that purports to create abundance and prosperity in actuality is creating some dangerous kinds of scarcity.

Early materialist philosophers of Europe, who claimed that all reality was ultimately reducible to hard material things called atoms, had trouble explaining the more ephemeral reality that we call mind or consciousness. Some decided that, if matter were the most basic reality or phenomenon of the world, then mind must be a secondary result of matter, a derivative or second-order reality which they called an "epiphenomenon."

Money is like an "epiphenomenon." Real wealth comprises the fundamental goods on which human, as well as animal and plant life depend. Wealth by this definition then, consists of the basic soils, water, sunlight, air, plants, and minerals of the planet. Money, on the other hand, is an extremely useful, but often elusive human construction. Each currency's value rests totally upon our collective "belief" or confidence in it.

What is money? What is wealth? How do they differ? Through the 1970s, investment on the stock markets of Wall Street was primarily used to finance productive enterprises that created jobs and goods for a consumer society.

By the early 1990s, a much higher percentage of the stock market investment represented pure speculation, money invested without direct links to productivity. Ph.D. and author David Korton writes: "When financial assets and transactions grow faster than growth in the output of real wealth, it is a strong indication that the global economy is getting sick. A study by McKinsey and Company found that from 1980 to 1992 financial assets in the developed countries of the OECD grew twice as fast as their underlying economies and bullishly predicted that future financial growth would be three times real output growth."[1] Stock prices lost relation to the productive assets in which one invested and rested upon the *confidence* that stock values would rise, and profits could be made on their sale. This historical development illustrates how money and wealth diverge, and how one can accumulate money without increasing wealth.

Money became a sort of "epiphenomenon" purportedly directly linked to "wealth," but increasingly unrelated to wealth. As distant memories of the stock market crash of the early twentieth century remind us, this kind of money was "in the mind" of those on whose confidence it depended.

Once we see that wealth forms the basic reality of our economic world and money forms an elusive kind of "epiphenomenon," some paradoxes of our modern situation become clearer. One such paradox is that money in our present-day world is being used to create not wealth but scarcity.

Seeds: Creating Scarcity with Money

If we look at wealth as the natural resources, biodiversity, natural life, clean air and water that make up the basic elements on which our lives depend and if we were to do an inventory of the state of this basic real wealth, we would see more clearly that our present Western economy, in significant ways, destroys wealth more than it creates wealth. Our Western economy, in fact, creates a variety of kinds of wealth scarcities. An inventory of fresh water, for example, would reveal an increasing shortage of potable water as aquifers shrink and rivers and underwater tables are contaminated. An inventory of soils would reveal massive loss of fertile topsoil through erosion and the destruction of soil's long-range productive capacity through microbe-killing chemical fertilizers and other agricultural chemicals. Uncontaminated air, essential for our own healthy intake of life-giving oxygen and also for the health of our planet, decreases in quality and availability each year for the majority of the world's population. Part of this is due to the 19.92 tons of CO_2 per capita released by the United States annually while the rest of the world's average contribution to this kind of contamination is 3.97 tons per capita.[2] And sunlight, essential for the growth of plant life, is compromised by the depletion of the ozone layer which replaces the benign sunlight filtered gently through the various layers of our planet's atmosphere with a sunlight high in destructive radiation.

This very limited kind of inventory, without mentioning the unprecedented extinction rates of the wild plants and animals of the planet, reveals a worrisome decline in the real wealth on which our life on the planet depends. Is this just a result of poor planning? Is it purely accidental? Or is it the logical consequence of the economic and philosophical principles foundational to our Western ways, to the life game we have chosen to play — a game of accumulation of money and things, not real wealth.

In reality, our current economic model creates four critical types of scarcity. What we do about these scarcities may determine whether the human experiment as we know it will survive the present century.

1. The dynamic, growth-oriented, expansion of the present economic model produces the *environmental scarcity* described above. But this is just the first kind of wealth decline that our economic model creates.

2. It produces what we could call a *planned competitive scarcity* as aggressively competitive marketing in combination with expanded intellectual property rights from the North actually eliminate access to traditional sources of wealth in the South.

3. A perceived consumer scarcity, which we could call the *scarcity of unfulfilled desire,* is being created by media campaigns gauged to create new consumer "needs" which are reaching every impoverished corner of the earth through television. Our current game cannot, presumably, work if the world's population ever grows satisfied with the possessions it has.

4. All of the mechanisms that together cause these first three scarcities conspire to create the fourth scarcity, what we call *poverty,* as they concentrate money wealth in the hands of ever fewer individuals, corporations, and shareholders who reside principally, though not exclusively, in the North.[3]

The case of *environmental scarcity* is relatively clear. The extent of our ability to create basic scarcity is well illustrated by Jared Diamond's example of the present-day Inuit people of northern Alaska. Though the Inuit are one of the most isolated peoples in the world, Western industrial practices have created an acute scarcity of healthy food in Inuit society. According to Diamond, many of the Inuit, whose primary food sources are whales, seals, and seabirds that eat fish and mollusks, now have recorded blood mercury levels "in the range associated with acute mercury poisoning, while the levels of toxic PCBs in Inuit mothers' breast milk fall in a range high enough to classify the milk as 'hazardous waste.'"[4] This drastic example of how our manipulation and abuse of the environment creates crucial scarcities in food, water, clean air, and the basic soil and animal resources on which we depend is, according to Diamond, just the tip of the iceberg.

What, though, is *planned competitive scarcity?* There is the notorious case of the Nestle Corporation's effort to convince poor mothers around the world that their baby formula was necessary for infant health. The formula was unnecessary and, for most, economically inaccessible as a substitute for readily available breast milk.

But today creation of planned competitive scarcity is closely tied to two powerful realities of the twenty-first century: monopolistic corporate practices and the use of patents. Let's look at the example of the Mixtec native seeds of Tierra Colorada Apoala.

For centuries, Mixtec families have passed down proven varieties of seeds, the product of centuries of experimentation and research, family to family, grandparents to sons, daughters, and grandchildren. Recently, researchers in just one municipality identified over one hundred varieties of the thirty or so races of native corn that still exist in the state of Oaxaca.[5] There is seed for corn that produces in dry weather, or in wet weather, in cold short seasons, and in long dependable summers. There are different corns for different uses. There is seed for corn to make tortillas, or to make *posole;* there are different corns for *atoles* and for *tamales.*[6]

Indigenous communities interchange, barter, buy, and sell this great diversity of seeds. The campesinos amply renew this seed stock most years when the harvest comes and they set aside seed for the coming year. Often they improve seed stock by careful selection of seeds from the plants with the most ears of corn, the best color, the most resistance to wind, etc. This method of cultivating and using corn has worked for many centuries.

Now, if I were a businessman who wanted to make money selling seeds that I produced in the United States into this indigenous community a thousand miles to the south of our border in this atmosphere of rich variety and availability of corn seed, what would I have to do? Either I would have to create seed that was extremely superior to the abundant native seed that is free or cheap, or I would have to find a way to create seed scarcity. I would have to create a *planned competitive scarcity.*

Some fifty years ago the seeds of the so-called "green revolution" seemed to accomplish the creation of such a scarcity.[7] Under special conditions these new seeds produced notably higher yields, but, at the same time, the special qualities and productiveness of these hybrid seeds diminished approximately 25 percent with each successive generation, creating a seed scarcity that obliged farmers to repurchase seed each year if they wished to obtain similar yields. The process of promoting hybrid seeds that were viable only the first year of planting, then, created a planned scarcity by eliminating an ancient and crucial option farmers had to obtain seed, namely, that of saving seeds from the harvest to plant again in the coming year. Such a *planned competitive scarcity* is usually created when a commercial enterprise uses various techniques to eliminate competing products from the range of choices of potential consumers. In this case, the hybrid seed eliminated the seed saved by the farmer himself as a product that could compete each spring with the seed that seed companies had available for sale.

Even though farmers in our area of the Mixteca Alta experimented with green revolution seeds purchased or initially provided free by government programs, for the most part they went back to their own native seeds as yields from the new seeds quickly degenerated in the difficult climate and soils of the region. The new seeds, in addition, did not have the special flavors for the myriad corn dishes traditional in indigenous cuisine. So in fact the scarcity planned by seed corporations achieved only partial success.

Today, the approval of patents on life forms such as those on genetically modified (transgenic) corn has once again cleared the way for seed companies to create seed scarcity, if not improved seeds.[8] Corn genes that have been genetically modified by companies like Monsanto have been approved for patenting. These patented genes, when they pass to other varieties of corn through spontaneous and uncontrollable natural processes such as pollination by wind and insects, remain the property of those who own the patents. New plants developed from this combination become the property of the corporation whose modified genes they contain, and their seeds cannot be replanted without incurring financial obligations to the owner. These patented seeds create an actual seed scarcity because farmers cannot legally save seeds produced by corn they have grown. This scarcity can be remedied only by purchase from the owners of the patents. In the United States the technique of patenting genes has, in the case of soybeans, cotton and corn, successfully eliminated from the consumer options of U.S. farmers the free seed which for centuries has been available to them from their own harvests.

But patents are effective in creating this seed scarcity and dependence on patent owners only for a limited period of time. If I could create a seed that is sterile after its first planting then I could create a permanent seed scarcity and a permanent and exclusive market for my seed. And today such seeds have been patented in Canada and Great Britain. Popularly called "Terminator" seeds, they are completely sterile on second planting. Once marketed they will oblige seed purchasers to buy each year from the owners of the patents. Though these seeds are sterile, they still produce pollen which can cross with other plants of the same family. If they were to pass on their sterility by pollination to the Mixteca Alta's myriad varieties of native corn, they would have finally created the ultimate, durable, planned seed scarcity to replace the rich variety and availability of corn seed in Mixtec communities. And if they were to pass on this sterility to the *teocintle* plant, the wild ancestor of corn? Then, as we saw above, we would have created an extremely dangerous form of *planned competitive scarcity* by attacking the original biodiversity on which corn depends for its long-term viability.[9]

The thought, and now the technological reality, that we could turn around the rich fecundity of the only known planet gifted with abundant life and render that fecundity sterile in order to create money demonstrates how great the gap between money and wealth has become in our Western tradition.

Planned competitive scarcity sometimes manifests itself in unintentional side effects. One such unforeseen consequence already affects campesinos in Latin America and Asia. Mexican campesino women explain to us that the edible wild plants that grow only in and around the cultivated fields of corn and beans are an abundant source of free food for their families. These green, leafy foods, called *quelites* in Mexico, are rich in vitamins, minerals, and iron. But green revolution agriculture, sold as the answer to the world's food problems, with its high dependence on chemical fertilizers, pesticides, and herbicides eliminates *quelites* with its powerful herbicides. Not only does this create a new kind of food scarcity by eliminating an abundant supply of free food, it impoverishes diets. In Asia, when herbicides eliminated *quelites* from family diets and processing of rice reduced the food value of this Asian staple, vitamin A deficiencies began to cause significant rates of incurable blindness. In response, Western biotech experts have had to invent the highly touted genetically modified golden rice, which is high in vitamin A . . . and patented, to make up for the new scarcity of healthful foods in Asian countries.

One might object that we are confusing economically neutral technological improvements with intentional commercial strategies to monopolize markets. Doesn't a successful technological innovation always replace inferior technologies in the market? From a strictly technological or scientific perspective this may be true. But technological advance does not automatically improve the quality of life, and it can actually cause deterioration in the quality of life. That is why it is so important that with each new technological option that is presented to us, as we saw in the case of the computer, we carefully analyze what we want from this technology and whether its total effect will be positive or negative. We need to consider what its impact will be on the social, human, natural, and already extant technological environment into which it is introduced. But in our current economic climate, there is no such thing as a purely technological innovation, independent of commercial interests. In this climate it is impossible to separate technological innovation from efforts to eliminate competing options and create competitive scarcity. This marriage of technology and commerce has undermined the type of scientific and technological honesty that demands a careful assessment of objectives and the general impact of new technologies on our lives and the life of the planet.

Eliminating competing sources of basic products that can serve human and natural needs by *planned competitive scarcity* becomes an extremely risky proposition when combined with the *environmental scarcity* of things like reliable sources of potable water and safe food, which already threatens some of the basic resources needed to support human life on this planet.

Free Trade, Privatization, and the Scarcity Trap

The remaining two types of scarcity, perceived scarcity and actual poverty, are, in our day, magnified by an economic and trade policy that is in vogue and that is mercilessly pushed upon the world by its believers and the institutions they control, including the World Trade Organization, the World Bank, the International Monetary Fund, and recent U.S. administrations. Its key concepts are called "free trade" and "market liberalization."

Free trade and market liberalization have been sold to the United States and world public under a number of guises. One of the most common half-truths being marketed is that free trade and market liberalization equal democracy. University of Chicago economist Milton Friedman is credited with being one of the first to equate what he called "economic freedom," or unregulated economies for international corporations, with "political freedom" when he needed to explain why the imposition of "free markets" in the dictator Pinochet's Chile required so much political repression.[10]

Unfortunately, free trade, as modeled by international trade agreements such as the North American Free Trade Agreement (NAFTA) exists not so much as a democratic development model that aims to improve economic conditions for all, but as a technique to allow the continuance of an economic model that demands continuous growth —

growth in profits at the same time as growth in resource depletion and contamination. Without growth, the current economic system, it is thought, cannot thrive.

But free trade exacerbates the two kinds of scarcity that we have already described. First, our economic system greased by free trade, through encouraging and justifying unmeasured and unsustainable consumption and contamination, creates a scarcity of the basic wealth of the planet — our air, water, soils, and sunlight. Second, *planned competitive scarcity*, by extending patents and legally enforceable monopoly corporate rights, as in the case of the genetically modified seeds, to an ever wider area of the world economy, reduces access to the basic goods of life so as to oblige the consumers of the world to purchase from international corporations predominantly based in the North.

In addition, the use of newly opened international borders to "dump" excess product from the North into Third World markets, for example, the dumping of U.S. corn in Mexico at prices below the cost of production (technically not permitted under World Trade Organization rules) is undermining campesino production around the world. In Mexico it is creating a dependence on corn from the North and on the exporters and processors who, instead of passing these low prices on to consumers, take advantage of families' new dependence on imports to skim ever higher profits from markets such as the Mexican tortilla market. In spite of corn prices 50 percent lower than before NAFTA, the price of tortillas has risen 700 percent in the NAFTA years.[11]

The creation of these two types of scarcity by itself would constitute an extremely dangerous scarcity game both environmentally and socially. One thousand scientists who met in late 2006 in India concluded that we are passing the point of no return with regard to the consequences of the environmental impact of our industrial emissions.[12] And when we consider the social impacts of these scarcities we create, we need to ask ourselves, "How long will the increasing population of the world's developing nations permit the nations of the North to exploit them?"

But in addition to all of this, the free trade model accelerates the creation of two added types of scarcity, the *scarcity of "unfulfilled desire"* and the scarcity we call *poverty*.

Part of the logic of "free trade" as it is conceived today, is to create a demand for the U.S. lifestyle and products around the globe.[13] But as television and its global marketing penetrate to the poorest corners of the globe, with its promotion of consumption and extravagance, the poor are watching from the sidelines. The newly created desires for the neatly and deceptively packaged U.S. and European way of life, however, will largely remain impossible to fulfill. A new and growing gap is created between what people are taught to desire and what in reality they will be able to obtain: a *scarcity of "unfulfilled desire."* These unfulfilled desires and expectations of a world population, half of whom live on less than $2 a day, create an explosive potential for social violence and revolution. These desires, the majority of which cannot be fulfilled, spawn a new type of resentment among an ever poorer majority. We may indeed be forced to face off with the poor over access to the lifestyle that this brand of globalization wishes to sell. Do we really want a future of wars with the poor over access to these products and this lifestyle?

There are alternatives. We need to be aware of them and consciously choose them.

Unfortunately, instead of building alternatives to this kind of bleak prospective future, we are creating more *actual poverty,* the fourth scarcity, with our current "liberalized" market and trade-based creed. The present economic model is successfully concentrating the money wealth of the world in the hands of a few Northern countries and a handful of powerful, wealthy individuals in the Global South. As it does so, as the Mixtec understanding of economics would predict, others are left with little or nothing. Real poverty levels and the gap between rich and poor have grown across Latin America and in the United States as well.[14] U.S. foreign and trade policy is creating the scarcity we call *poverty.* And all the while these same poor who are watching Western TV shows and movies, witness live in their own countries this concentration of money in the hands of the few. Money in Latin America is concentrated in gated communities and shopping malls, which are moneyed ghettos surrounded by slum zones of tin shacks and street vendors. And from the TV images, the United States appears to be one more homogenized moneyed ghetto. While most of the U.S. poor remain hidden from the view of the middle and upper classes, we still see some of them, the homeless, in every city, sleeping on park benches, and getting food out of dumpsters or at food kitchens. How long will the patience of the world's 3 billion poor last?

If the Mixtecs are right, and we live in a zero sum world in this twenty-first century of Western society, in a world where if some have too much some will be left with little or nothing, winning this complicated free trade scarcity game may not only be dangerous for the rest of the world, but for U.S. citizens as well.

Free Trade: Creating Money and Poverty

The Mixtec people celebrating in Tierra Colorada have to this point largely insulated themselves from the forces that create the scarcities we have talked about. They have not become dependent on external markets or on fertilizers or food purchased from other countries. They have not, for the most part, been lured into consumer dreams that are impossible to fulfill. They have remained to a large degree self-sufficient.

But across Mexico and the rest of Latin America others have not been so fortunate and the economic pressures of the "liberalized economy" and free trade have made them poorer. How is "free trade" creating increasing numbers of poor people?

Though the Western development model and its successes in Europe and the United States have been built upon protectionism, today the industrial and commercial base in the United States has grown confident that it can now dominate economies of the Global South, eliminating competition from within developing countries and creating a scarcity of local products, which obliges the huge populations of the South to buy from the North. Under the guise of free trade, variations of the strategies used to try to create seed scarcity in the Mixteca Alta now function in all aspects of the economic life of the Global South. This leads to a net flow annually of billions of dollars from South to North — quantities that dwarf all so-called "aid" and development programs from the developed North.[15]

Privatization is another tool that forms an integral element in free trade strategies. Large corporations now control "markets," which no longer function according to dynamic interaction between demand and supply as described by classical economists. But these large corporations cannot create the necessary scarcity of local goods and services in the Global South as long as their governments protect their populations from the forces of the so-called "market" by subsidizing health care, education, or basic industries. So the large corporations pressure governments to get out of business, sell off para-state industries, and eventually privatize all services to their populations, including health and education, and allow foreign firms to compete in their markets to supply these service needs in the South. When this process is completed, the dependence of the South on the North will also have been completed, and money will flow unfettered from South to North. This, of course, creates money in the Global North, but poverty in the Global South.

Privatization schemes that put basic necessities of all of us on the market have their limitations, however. For instance, the thought that the 3 billion people of the world's population who live on less than $2 a day would happily and peacefully die of thirst, if priced out of a privatized water market by the elimination of government services, can only be sustained by someone with very little experience outside the walls of academia or outside the Washington, DC, Beltway. But many of those seriously pushing the privatization of, for instance, water, as a way to solve the water scarcity problem know exactly what they are after. The most efficient water delivery systems in the world continue to be public, though there are disastrously wasteful systems both private and public. But one thing reigns universal in this across the board. The cost of water always has risen dramatically with privatization.[16]

Proponents of free trade will continue to argue that they are creating wealth and abundance, not scarcity and poverty. While data exists claiming improvements in services to the world's poor over the last generation, Mexico's example puts such claims in doubt. The model of trade and market liberalization began to have a strong effect on Mexico in the late 1980s. Since that time Mexico has seen a 1400 percent increase in the cost of the basic market basket (consisting of thirty-five food items, the estimated minimum need of a Mexican family) while the minimum salary increased by only 300 percent, leaving present-day Mexicans with a 73 percent drop in buying power. According to studies done by analysts at the Autonomous University of Mexico,[17] while in 1987 the minimum salary would buy thirty-one of the thirty-five items in the basic market basket, today it suffices to purchase only five items or up to 16 percent of the necessary minimum. In addition, during the same period there has been a constant increase in unemployment and a concurrent decrease in the quality of jobs, with a 59 percent decrease in jobs in the larger businesses and industries of the country. Today half of the working population is employed in micro-businesses, often selling on the streets, and a third in the informal sector. At the same time there was a loss of 1.8 million people from the rural working population, principally through migration, and in spite of the lower workforce, an increase in rural unemployment of 173 percent.[18]

What happened to all the people displaced by low agricultural prices and poverty is a story of interest to North Americans. They migrated, and they can be traced by the dramatic changes in money transfers from Mexican workers in the United States to their families and home communities in Mexico. In 1995 these workers sent back to Mexico a total of $4.2 billion. In 2005, even though wages had not increased in the

U.S., they sent back an astounding five times that amount ($20.8 billion), suggesting that the economic policies connected with "free trade" and liberalization have helped to create a 400 percent to 500 percent increase in poverty-induced migration to the United States.[19] By far the most striking outcomes of free trade are this massive increase in migration and the huge amount of money it have created for the corporate proponents of free trade, and for the small, elite class of billionaires and millionaires in Mexico and around the world.

This process of pauperization has had very specific effects on rural Mexico, especially in communities that, unlike Tierra Colorada, have become dependent on international goods and markets. In Mexico, low prices of imported corn subsidized by U.S. taxpayers have reduced market prices that farmers receive by 50 percent. Privatized production of fertilizers by market monopolies has led to 300 percent increases in the cost of fertilizers these farmers must buy.[20] This has drastically reduced or even eliminated small and medium farm income and forced millions of rural people to emigrate to the cities or to the United States. Farmers who remained tied to these market systems that increased their costs of production and drastically lowered the prices for their produce sank into poverty. In the case of Mexican coffee farmers, many of whom specialized in coffee production to the exclusion of traditional food crops, this often meant severe hunger and desperate marches north.

As we mentioned above, U.S. politicians and citizens wonder why we have a problem with illegal immigration and what we can do to effectively "control" the massive tide of people crossing into the United States, approximately five hundred of whom die in the attempt each year, according to official figures, in the southwestern deserts of California, Arizona, and New Mexico. Politicians and others will not find any reliable answers unless they look at the kind of new poverty that NAFTA has created in rural Mexico, and so far they are not looking at their own contribution to the problem. Nor has this free trade process led to the promised cheap basic consumer prices. Under the new dynamics of the privatized corporate market, the cost of corn tortillas, as sold to the people who invented corn, as we saw, has risen 700 percent to 800 percent over the last eleven years. When we consider that the tortilla makes up the majority of the calories in the Mexican diet, we can better imagine the effects of the scarcity created by these privatized prices on the Mexican people. Poverty has risen during NAFTA to 50 percent in the general population and up to 85 percent in rural areas. Because of the human spirit that ever seeks survival, you will see more and more of these people in your cities and in your suburbs, refugees from economically besieged and decimated lands. This concomitant concentration of wealth and increase of poverty provides a clear example of the Mixtec principle of the limited good. When some have too much, as does the United States as a nation, many, like the poor of Mexico and Central America, do not have basic necessities. This effectively propels migration from the Global South to the North.

Never before in the history of the planet has any society possessed the capability to create scarcity of basic wealth and scarcity of local goods and production on a scale such as that attained by Western societies and their international corporations today. Are we unwittingly creating our own demise as we create a scarcity that is neither ecologically nor socially viable, in the name of that epiphenomenon we call "money"?

But the people of Tierra Colorada are perhaps still more in touch with the basic wealth of the planet. Because they have maintained some independence from the forces that now concentrate money in the hands of the few, because they have chosen, instead, sustainable use of local sources of natural fertilizers and pest control, native seeds and modest, inexpensive technologies, they have not joined the ranks of the hungry. Instead, in Tierra Colorada this night, food is abundant. In the dedication Mass, the priest declares "fiesta" the eighth sacrament because it creates joy, sharing, and community. After the fireworks light up the dark, cold mountain sky and the ritual dances and offerings are completed, after we join in the Salsa, the Cumbia, and learn traditional Oaxacan dances to the sound of Miguel's band, we leave the well-fed village of Tierra Colorada with its people dancing on into the night.

Chapter Six

Objection!

Romanticizing Indigenous and U.S. Cultures

Romanticizing Traditionalism and Poverty?

By now some will be objecting that we are romanticizing the indigenous campesino life and culture we are visiting, and perhaps that we are romanticizing poverty itself. First, let us look at some of what Mixtec people say about their own life and poverty, and then let's consider the possibility that we perhaps are in much greater danger of romanticizing our own American way of life.

Water is scarce in the village of San Isidro Tilantongo. As we walked along the road from Fermina and Jesús's house toward the tiny town center, we passed the white, barren subsoil of an eroded field that now lay fallow and useless for the planting of most crops. On the other side of the road, uphill from us, we could see reforested areas with new shade and new soils accumulating with the rotting leaf mold the forests provided.

We came to a pair of sturdy rock troughs full with clear, cool water and glistening in the arid sunshine. "This is water from one of the three springs we have in the village," Jesús explained. "One trough is for the animals' use and the other is for human use, where we can fill our buckets and water jars."

"We don't have much water," he continued. "But we don't need much because we don't have a sewer system."

"We don't have a sewer system!" The implications of that simple statement began to race through my mind. "You mean," I thought, as we continued up the dusty path to the tiny village square, "that if someone

Mixtec women organizing for change

had come in here twenty years ago and said you need to pull yourselves out of this poverty and helped you put in a sewer system, San Isidro would long ago have exhausted its water supplies and would no longer exist! Right?"

Clearly, water-based sewer systems would be a suicidal option for villages such as San Isidro. But the Mexican government officially measures poverty by the absence of sewer systems and the presence of dirt floors in rural communities. Being "poor" means having no sewer system and no cement floor.

Later I learned that Jesús was fighting against putting a sewer system in the municipal center of Santiago Tilantongo.

"Everyone is accusing me of being anti-progress," he laughed one day. "But the system will be very expensive and will serve only the 1 percent of the population that lives close enough to be connected to it. Furthermore, if the treatment facilities for the waste are like in a couple of neighboring villages, within a few years they will cease to function, and this stinky human waste will be piling up in some *arroyo*. Anyway, it will use an additional ten thousand liters of water a day that we don't have! How stupid to foul the little pure water we have just to get rid of our human waste. We need better solutions than the flush toilet, like the ecological toilets we build in the communities. But then we would still be 'poor'!"

Various times I have heard indigenous people express the thought that having an outhouse or a dirt floor has nothing to do with being "poor." "Poverty," they would say, "is not having land to plant our crops, not having schools for our children, not having access to medical care. Yet they want to convince us that we are poor and pitiable because we have customs and ways of life that have served for millennia but are not like that of urban people. Many of the ways we do things are better for our life here, more practical, and represent a knowledge that has been shown to work by our ancestors."

When I listen to the hard-headed logic of Jesús about flush toilets, for instance, I see that this is far from an attempt to romanticize poverty or traditional ways. It is a stubborn insistence upon basing our concepts of "progress" and a "good life" on careful analysis of basic problems and their solutions, on what we want out of life and what will most likely get us to what we truly want life to be. By this logic, valuing tried traditional ways and choosing simple, accessible technologies over technologies we in the United States might see as essential is not romanticizing.

The Mexican government, and probably many of us in the North also, would like to keep the question of "poverty" simple. If the Mexican government can define poverty as dirt floors and outhouses, then for every cement floor it helps construct it can count one poor person out of Mexico's astounding poverty figures.[1] If we in the North can reduce solutions for poverty to technologies to produce more food or make more consumer goods available, we can justify our relatively extravagant lifestyle and say that by producing more food and consumer goods, we have fulfilled our duty to the poor.

But if I were to claim that indigenous campesino life is not necessarily poverty but may in fact represent a good and viable way of life as long as basic needs that indigenous people themselves decide on are met, I might be accused of romanticizing indigenous cultures.

Truthfully, I think there is much more danger in romanticizing our own culture in the North. When we do romanticize it, we do so at a much greater cost to the world socially, economically, and environmentally. When we hold up our own way of life as a model for the world and the measure of the good life, we ignore a great deal about how this way of life has been attained and maintained as well as many of its weaknesses. We also tempt the remainder of the world to join us on a dangerously unsustainable path to the future. So before we move on in the next chapter to looking at some other basic differences between Mixtec values and our own, let's look at some of the ways we romanticize our own history and way of life.

Why Mexico Has Never "Made It"

Last year, my wife, Kathy, and I were sitting around the kitchen table of the Nebraska farmhouse of our friends, Mary and Virgil, with a group of farmers and former farmers talking about the effects free trade was having on Mexican farmers. As the conversation was winding down, one thoughtful farmer asked, "Why do you think that Mexico has never made it like the United States? It certainly is a country with many natural resources."

I thought for a minute. I liked that question and had some ideas. I began, "Clearly you'd definitely have to say that corruption is one of the things that has always held Mexico back. The corruption is huge and, it seems, always has been. But there's another interesting thing to consider." And I began to explain the theories of liberation theologian Pablo Richard, that all of the civil wars in the Americas, including our own civil war, had been fought not primarily over issues such as slavery but over free trade and protectionism.

In the United States, according to Richard, the protectionist North won. And so the well-protected small industries of the North flourished and determined the history of the United States as a prosperous indus-trialized country. On the other hand, in every case, the civil wars of the Latin American countries had different victors. In each case, the free traders won, and the economies that resulted depended on exporting raw materials to the international market instead of developing a domestic industrial base. Prices of these raw materials, for example, cotton, minerals, and forest products, were always unstable and out of the control of the providing countries. In fact, the price of raw materials relative to manufactured goods kept declining through the years for the countries that depended on exporting raw materials.

In addition, according to Richard, the Latin American export-oriented model depended on the availability of vast amounts of very cheap labor, just as the economy of the U.S. South depended on cheap slave labor. Thus, it became essential for these economies to maintain a large and basically poor working class that could provide this cheap labor force. All of these factors together determined that Latin American economies would be relatively poor, dependent on international markets they could not control, and with a domestic population with a vast divide between a small wealthy elite who owned the farms and mines that produced the countries' exports and a large poor population that supplied the cheap labor for their extraction.

"Mexico has always found itself trapped in this same dynamic with virtually all of the rest of Latin American countries whose victorious elites opted to be 'free traders'," I concluded.

My listeners were impressed with this answer. And I continued to feel somewhat smug about how the evening had gone until, as we drove back toward the Mexican border the next morning, I suddenly realized — on further reflection — that I had made the same mistake again!

"Damn!" I said to myself. "Once again I let us off the hook. I left everyone there with a reinforced argument for a common and extremely dangerous American misperception: that the solution to the world's problems is for everyone to try to be more like us!" We have already seen that we would need many more earths than the one we have now if we were to feed on a worldwide scale the ravenous consumerism we maintain in the United States.

In fact, the most important thing that Latin Americans have taught me over the past thirty years is that this misperception, so common to most of us North Americans, is possible only because of the romanticized understanding that most white, middle-class Americans have of our country and its history. Latin Americans will frequently point out that many of the things that make for U.S. prosperity are not replicable and probably shouldn't be replicated — twenty-five U.S. military invasions and interventions in Latin America, for instance.

De-Romanticizing U.S. Culture:
Our Nineteenth-, Twentieth-, and
Twenty-First-Century Resource Wars

In 1987 our oldest daughter, Erica, graduated from college and went to El Salvador for a year as a volunteer in a school run by the Sisters of the Assumption. Not long afterward she wrote that she had left the school and had begun working with Salvadoran refugees returning from camps in Mesa Grande, Honduras. Her letters told of accompanying the returning Salvadorans from a tiny village called Copapayo. The U.S.-supported Salvadoran army had massacred the majority of the villagers a few years earlier, but the returning campesinos hung white flags from the trees to deter the hovering Salvadoran army helicopters and began life anew. Erica accompanied them as they first went to the remains of the village center and began digging in the dirt. They unearthed pots and basic tools hastily buried years earlier by the fleeing survivors of the massacre. One man unearthed the carefully preserved white baptismal dress of his little girl, who had been killed by the soldiers. Then they dug up the church bell, which had also been buried in their flight. They hung it from an improvised cross-beam, rang it, and called the returning villagers to pray the rosary together.

As we read more about the U.S. history in El Salvador and continued receiving our daughter's letters, it became clear that the massacre at Copapayo was by no means unique. It also became clear that the United States, in spite of denials by our government officials, well knew of these massacres. Yet the United States kept pouring more aid, military advisors, bombs, and aircraft into the country.

By 1989 Erica was still working in El Salvador, now with families displaced by the war in a shantytown on the edge of the capital city of San Salvador. We knew that the guerrilla opposition, the FMLN, had begun a new offensive near the capital city, and we were deeply concerned about our daughter. Then one day the phone rang, and it was Erica. She was calling from the shantytown of tin and cardboard shacks where she lived and worked.

"Dad!" I heard her urgent voice. "The army is strafing and bombing this whole neighborhood of tin shacks. Nobody has any place to hide. Little kids are crying in the streets, not knowing if their parents are alive or dead. We at the parish are in one of the only sturdy buildings around and people are flocking here. We are giving medical assistance to the wounded. But you've got to try to get hold of the State Department and tell them to call the army off! These are U.S. bombs that are falling on us!"

"Are you all right?" I yelled back into the phone, feeling the fear rising in my stomach.

"I'm okay," she shouted back over the noise of the bombing. "It's ironic, the only things still working in the neighborhood are our TV, and hundreds of refugees hiding under beds are watching the Salvadoran president and the U.S. ambassador saying that reports that our neighborhood is being strafed and bombed are false. And the other thing still working is this pay phone I'm calling from. See what you can do!"

The click of the phone hanging up shut us into days of silent worrying and wondering. Calls to the State Department were ineffective. Then the news arrived of the massacre of the six Jesuit priests at the University in San Salvador and their housekeeper, Elba, and her daughter, who had been involved in activities of Erica's parish. We got hold of a Sister whom Erica had stayed with a few days earlier.

"Erica has gone to evacuate people from the parish neighborhood to safer ground," she told us. "Just pray as you've never prayed before."

Then came reports that the parish building where she and the parish team and refugees had been staying had been bombed. Then, finally, anguished days later, a call from Erica. The fighting was over, for now.

A year later, along with two of our younger children, Dominic and Teresa, I was in the shantytown by the railroad tracks where Erica worked. It was the anniversary of the massacre of the Jesuits, and we were practicing songs for the next day's Mass at the university. Then I noticed whispered messages being passed from ear to ear on the other side of the parish room. The meeting broke up quickly, and Erica informed me that the message was from the *muchachos,* the "boys," as the guerrillas were called by neighborhood people. A new offensive was to begin that night and everyone needed to be off the streets by 8:00 p.m. Erica and I made plans about what to do when the fighting started. I would take the younger kids to the center of town to a designated place, and she would go to the parish to try to help with the inevitable crowd of wounded and refugees. We said as little as possible to the younger kids. They would learn what this was about soon enough.

A little later as I lay down in the small bed in the makeshift room a few feet from the railroad tracks that ran through the shantytown, I could have kicked myself for bringing the little kids into this mess. But then I couldn't take another time like last year not knowing for days whether Erica was alive or dead. I drifted off.

U.S. Military Invasions and Interventions in Latin America

1831 — The Malvinas Islands

1845, 1848 — Mexico

1855, 1860, 1909, 1912, 1926, 1980s — Nicaragua

1898, 1961 — Cuba

1898 — Puerto Rico

1903 — Colombia/Panama

1915, 1995 — Haiti

1916, 1965 — Dominican Republic

1946 — Bolivia

1954 — Guatemala

1955 — Argentina

1973 — Chile

1980 — El Salvador

1981, 1989 — Panama

1983 — Granada

I awoke with a start. That was a train whistle! Light was pouring in around the cracks in the walls of the plywood room. It was morning. I sat up and listened for a moment. All seemed quiet outside the thin walls. I got up quickly and went out to the kitchen area. Erica had just returned from the parish.

"The U.S. Congress just cut military aid to Salvador last night, so the FMLN postponed the offensive," she announced. The tension began to drain out of my body. The now sun-drenched neighborhood of cardboard and tin seemed to relax too. Everyday noises of people washing clothes, clanging pots, dogs barking, children laughing had a new beauty to them in the cool air of the morning.

Then I felt a deep anger rising inside me. "By what right did those wealthy politicians in plush chairs in the U.S. Congress decide the life and death of people in this faraway Salvadoran shantytown!" The anger has continued to simmer in me. It has also helped me to understand what Latin Americans are saying about the United States.

In the 1980s U.S. military adventures were "making the world safe for democracy." The Salvadoran version of this, with its massacres of the poor, was a representative sample of this type of "democracy." But in reality, to Latin Americans this and other U.S. actions in the Global South were and continue to be seen as resource wars. Though El Salvador's resources were minimal, the Washington policy elite considered victory over what was a politically diverse and nationalistic insurgency critical to maintaining hegemony and, therefore, access to the resources and markets in the rest of Latin America.

To Latin Americans, it seems that U.S. wealth and power are built upon interventions, massacres, and wars like that in El Salvador aimed primarily at controlling access to the resources of our neighbors to the south. They can count at least twenty-five such invasions or interventions of U.S. forces in Latin America since we occupied the Malvinas Islands in 1831.[2] Virtually all of these military efforts assured access to Latin American resources for U.S. political and economic ends. Of course the largest is well remembered by Mexicans: the forced "sale" of half of Mexico to the United States, as a result of the Mexican-American War that we already know was provoked by President Polk. That enriched the United States by the seven states of New Mexico, Arizona, Colorado, Nevada, California, Utah, and parts of Oregon. Nothing to sneeze at, economically speaking. And, of course, this says nothing about non-Latin American interventions, such as in the Philippines and Hawaii.

Mexico hasn't "made it" like the United States has in good part because it has never learned to successfully carry out such wars to colonize other people's resources. When we cease to romanticize the American Way of Life and see to what extent it is dependent upon resource wars, the reasons for our economic successes become less replicable. And the resource wars continue in this twenty-first century, as in Iraq.

I had indeed missed another good opportunity with the Nebraskan farmers to share what Latin Americans had taught me. A good bit of our economic success and Mexico's lack of it is due to our military and political interventions to control Latin American resources. This is not, presumably, something that we would want Mexico to imitate.

María's Story

But to Latin Americans, we negatively impact the South not only because of our penchant for resource wars. We also externalize a great deal of the cost of unsustainable U.S. lifestyles on the people of the South.

María's story, written by Maryknoll Sister Dee Smith, who works with migrant AIDS patients near the Guatemalan-Mexican border, shows the dark underbelly of these costs that we externalize to the South.

We meet up with María and her sisters daily in the streets and highways of Mexico and Central America.

My name is María and I was ten years old when the Sandinistas tried for a new dream for us. My father, Don Timoteo, died fighting the Contras, and my mother was left a widow with six of us to feed. Despite the efforts of the Sandanistas over the years, the situation in Nicaragua slowly became worse, and Hurricane Mitch, in 1998, finished off our little village and left us worse than ever.

I married quickly when I was fifteen years old and had a child immediately. I felt I would be one less to feed for my mother. Tomás, my son, is now twenty years old but I don't know where he is because he left home for Costa Rica when he was thirteen to look for his uncle and cousin since they live and work there. I looked at my mother one day, and I knew I would have to help her. My husband stayed one year with me, but his drinking led to many fights. They say he left for Costa Rica also, but I don't care what happened to him. I drifted into the city looking for work. I was seventeen at the time, and a nice lady offered me a job in Guatemala City as a waitress serving in a restaurant. I had never been to Guatemala, and the woman said I would earn a lot of money to send to my family. She said four other young women were traveling with me. Two were from Honduras and two from El Salvador.

When we arrived in Guatemala City, Doña Rosa kept my documents for safekeeping and showed me to my room. It didn't look like much, and there was only one bed. I wasn't going to share a room with my friends, Juana and Julia from El Salvador and Martita and Betty from Honduras. We each had our own bedroom.

We quickly realized that it was a nightclub and not a restaurant. As you can imagine, I was frightened, and more so when Doña Rosa said I had to be "kind" to the men who came to the club. I had to serve drinks and then accept to have sex with whoever came along.

One day, after three years of being a slave with Doña Rosa, a man came and told me that I had to move to another place, as the men were tired of me and my friends; they said they were bored and needed new girls.

The following night, Juana, Martita, and me were put into a truck and taken to Honduras to another nightclub. The nightmare began again, and we cried a lot. I had begun to change: I could feel it inside myself. I was angry all the time and needed to drink to push down the pain and to keep away the memory of my mother and the rest of the family. What did they care that I wasn't the successful secretary I told them I was, as long as the money kept arriving every month.

It was during this time that Juana suggested that we run away and try to get to Mexico, where she said women could get good bar work and then travel to the United States of America, get work, and live a wonderful life — even bring up the family later. Martita and I were a bit scared but trusted Juana. It took us six months of working the bars along the Pacific coast of Guatemala to save enough money to get to Tapachula, Mexico, and from there to hire a *coyote* to take us to the USA.

I was now thirty-four years old and had my dream of going to the United States and starting anew. Six months ago I was ready to go through Mexico to the States, when Juana told me she had met Betty again, but she was in a hospital in Tapachula. The story was sad; Betty had tried to jump the train in Tapachula to go up north, when two men in their rush to get on the train pushed Betty under the wheels, and she lost both legs.

Betty was crying all the time saying how she couldn't go back to Honduras with no legs and had no way to help her family. Juana cried with her but had no solution. I too was sad for Betty, but more worried about myself. I had been losing weight and had sores in my mouth and around my vagina. I didn't feel good and told Juana to go ahead on the train, and I'd follow her when I felt better. That was two months ago and I am still in the bar, feeling worse everyday. I have nowhere to go and no one to help me. People have started to say I have AIDS. I heard today that maybe I can go to a hospice in Guatemala to be taken care of. I don't care what happens to me now. All of my dreams are finished.

We could simply conclude that María ran into some nasty people. She didn't run into the youth gangs that attacked a young Honduran man I met on the streets of Oaxaca the other day. These gangs tortured the young Honduran with pliers on his ears, pulling off the whole bottom half of one ear in their attempt to find out where he had hidden his traveling money. Nor was she victimized by the narco-traffickers who now have joined with the *coyotes,* who traffic in getting people across borders, and the prostitution rings that traffic in both young women and young men. These three groups are now building their own "hotels" on the Guatemalan-Mexican border to hold migrants who are heading north until border-crossing times. And what do these stories have to do with us? Actually, they have a considerable amount to do with us.

The costs of the U.S. dominance that makes our standard of living possible are deeply felt south of our border today. The free trade policies mentioned above — designed primarily to take advantage of the asymmetrical economies in North and South America and the abundant cheap labor costs of the South, are destroying domestic production in the South and creating new economic refugees streaming north to find a way to survive. This amounts to externalizing onto Latin America the costs of supporting a lifestyle that consumes a grossly disproportionate percentage of the world's resources. With about 4.67 percent of the world's population, the United States possesses 25.4 percent of the world's net worth, or over five times our share,[3] and total energy consumption rates reflect a similar disproportion.[4] How much energy does one upper-middle-class U.S. household consume compared to that of entire villages in most of the world?

The fact is that these migrant experiences are part of a systematic corruption of once stable lifestyles across the Americas. And U.S. military and political interventions, as well as trade and economic policies, share a significant amount of the blame for this corruption. María and those like her leave Nicaragua, Honduras, El Salvador, Guatemala, and Southern Mexico partly because, throughout recent history, U.S. foreign policy makers, working in tandem with Latin American elites, have closed the path to change for the large mass of the poor in Latin America. We have done this in several ways.

During the past fifty years we have opposed and, in some cases, overthrown governments of change across the region, for instance, Nicaragua in 1855 and 1860, 1909, 1912, and 1926, Bolivia in 1946, Argentina and Guatemala in 1954, and the Dominican Republic in 1965. By selling such interventions to the good and generous people of the United

States as anti-communism or protection against "radical" regimes that threatened U.S. security, U.S. policymakers have blocked elected governments of change from moderate European-style socialist experiments in Chile, to reformist capitalist governments in Guatemala. The democratically elected president of Chile, Salvador Allende, was assassinated in 1973 during a CIA-backed coup. It was democratically elected Jacobo Arbenz in Guatemala in 1953. We are also suspects in the assassinations of President Jaime Roldós in Ecuador and Omar Torrijos in Panama for their loyalty to their countries' national interest over our own.[5]

And then there is our alleged participation in the assassinations and disappearances of the civilian opposition to military dictatorships across South America during the infamous "Operation Condor" of the 1970s and 1980s.[6] We have blocked labor reforms, land reforms, and attempts to challenge the vast concentration of wealth in the hands of the few, which is still today endemic to Latin American countries. In the process, U.S. policy has helped create some of the most repressive regimes Latin America has ever known and, in fact, has participated directly with such regimes in Argentina, Chile, El Salvador, and Nicaragua. It has also participated in the kidnapping, torture, and assassination of citizens opposing such regimes.

The U.S. public, in whose name these atrocities were committed and who paid for them with their taxes, were told, as we are told today about Iraq, that we were promoting "democracy." Our objective was neither to promote nor protect democracy in these foreign countries. Our primary objective was to maintain or create access to resources critical to supporting our lifestyles as well as to promote and protect U.S. corporate profits. In point of fact, we acted to destroy or undermine the democracies in these countries. But you can't just come out and tell the people that, can you? Those of us over fifty years of age have heard the sales pitch of wars as "promoting democracy" several times in our lifetimes, and some fifteen to twenty years later, we find out from "declassified" documents what our country's leaders were really up to when they told us we were promoting democracy.

Currently, U.S. policymakers push "free trade" agreements than *increase* rather that *decrease* the concentration of wealth within Latin American countries and create a flow of capital northward. This contributes to the destruction of rural economies and forces already poor masses to leave for the north, as we have seen.[7] The same politicians who crafted, promoted, and ultimately sold us the public policies that accelerated migration now blame the migrants themselves for fulfilling the natural consequences of free trade policies. The Bush administration at one point proposed sending 150,000 U.S. National Guard members to the U.S. border to stem the rising human tide flowing north.[8] We romanticize and sanitize all of this by calling this, along with the political, economic, and military policies that are responsible for the new waves of migration, "democracy building." The Marías of the Global South feel the consequences of our "romanticizing" most painfully.

But the game that we have allowed our U.S. political and foreign policy leaders to play has little to do with democracy.

Decades of U.S foreign and trade policy forced María into the migrant stream, and, as the stream grows, the migrants become more desperate and more cut off from their communities of origin — communities with their own cultures, mores, and social controls — and the migrant environment becomes more inhuman and violent.

The drug traffickers enter the scene, forcing migrants to become carriers. But the drug traffic is our creation also. It feeds almost exclusively on the insatiable North American appetite for escape through drugs. Without this demand, as Latin Americans are fond of pointing out, there would be no narco-traffickers.

The youth gangs of Central America and now of southern Mexico are also partly of our creation. They are run by Latino American youth formed in the gang culture in Los Angeles and Latin ghettos around our country. The poverty in our ghettos is part of the externalized costs of the economic conglomerates who dominate our country's wealth and increasingly concentrate that wealth, as in Latin America, in the hands of an ever shrinking elite.[9]

If we cease romanticizing our way of life in the North, we see that the Marías of the south pay with their stories and lives part of the externalized costs of our ability to live the way we do. If we get over romanticizing the "good life" we have created, we see how our lifestyles depend on the territories, resources, and markets of others — assured by wars and military interventions — to maintain their viability. And, as we will see in later chapters, we can then decide to do something about it.

Of course, even on its own merits, our lifestyle is not as rosy as we might like to think, if we take into account the stagnant poverty rates in our own country, the lack of adequate medical care for many, and the recent rise in infant mortality.[10] Add to that the psychic insecurities that make us heavily dependent on the drugs that create narco-trafficking across the poorer countries, to say nothing of the high rate of mental illness that, according to studies done on the Texas border, show us to have a considerably higher rate of mental illness than the campesino migrants who arrive at our border.

We really do a disservice to our country when we romanticize these facts and remain blind, as a people, to what the rest of the world can see quite clearly about the negative effects of our economic and political policies and our lifestyle on the world around us. We are, after all, basically a people of good will. And we are faced in recent years with the fact that we are disliked in much of the world without clearly understanding why.

This, of course, does not mean that our policies alone are to blame for the plight of the Marías of the world. Many Mexican officials are corrupt. Mexican border authorities are considered by most migrants to be much more vicious and dishonest than U.S. border officials. The indigenous cultures themselves, as we will see in the next chapter, have serious faults. We in the United States have many honest public servants, many generous and good-hearted people and communities. We are not romanticizing, however, when we point out that indigenous cultures have some values from which we not only can learn, but *need* to learn as we try to create a sustainable and peaceful future for ourselves and our neighbors around the world. And we need to be on guard against the all too tempting tendency to romanticize our own culture and our own way of life.

Chapter Seven

Culture and Violence

Who or What Is behind Indigenous Violence — and Our Own Violence?

If the Mixtec culture and its traditions and values can help us to reflect on our own culture, on how we value work and wealth, perhaps it can help us to reflect on something very basic: how we value human life.

The village of Santiago Amoltepec challenges all preconceptions. It is one of the poorest in all of Mexico and known for violent political disputes and struggles with its neighbors over community boundaries. Four religious Sisters who live there called for help in carrying out a walk for peace in this municipality, where fifteen people had been murdered over political disputes the past year and where house burnings had become frequent.

So three Maryknoll lay missioners, including myself, and three lay people from a Catholic diocesan human rights office set out a little before daylight for this remote village of the Mixteca Alta region of Oaxaca. Three hours later we left the last pavement behind. "It's about another hour or so to Amoltepec," said a woman we had picked up on the way. "Depending on how fast you go." Evidently, we weren't going fast enough over the rock-strewn pathways that served for roads. Three hours later we emerged from the dense pine forests into the village of Santa Cruz Itundujia, which clusters around two large stone church spires. For the next six hours we slowly labored through high, cold pine forest, passing small clusters of log and wooden plank homes. In the village of Chamisal we picked up six more local indigenous organizers and church people, and our expanded crew of nine arrived at the spectacular overlook of a breathtaking valley that fell precipitously to a blue-green ribbon of river far below. In the distance, towering spires

National hero Benito Juárez holds a white flag of peace during a heavily repressed popular uprising that left twenty-three dead in Oaxaca in 2006

of purple mountain ranges repeated themselves like endless shadows of one another as far as the eye could see.

The road descended toward the Pacific coast, and hours later, now in steaming tropical heat, we crossed the Río Verde, the ribbon of river we had seen from above, and began the last climb up barren brown mountainsides to our destination. We arrived at the first villages of the municipality of Amoltepec in dense darkness. Not a single light shone in the village. But Don Abdón, who served as our guide, found the house where one of the Sisters was staying. By flashlight in the darkness we greeted each other and made plans for the following day.

More violence had occurred in recent days between those in these outlying villages and those in the center of Amoltepec, and all sides were afraid to meet together to pray for peace, according to the original plan. So after deciding to divide into two groups for the next day's peace pilgrimage, we continued another half hour in the dark to the top of the mountain, where we came upon the brightly lit *municipio* of Santiago Amoltepec.

We slept that night on the cement floor of the new village church. The next morning as the sun rose orange over the endless rows of mountains, we gazed down on banks of clouds floating well below our mountain perch outside the small church. It seemed like an incongruous atmosphere for violence.

Disputes with neighboring villages over community boundaries are commonplace in the indigenous communities of Oaxaca. As my friend Fidel, who is now in charge of community lands in the town of Santiago Tilantongo, says, "Nobody really knows where the correct boundaries are." For decades, state and federal governments have allowed this ambiguity to continue, and they have even promoted disputes by giving out conflicting boundary information to keep communities distracted from the excesses of local, regional, and national political bosses or *caciques*.

But Amoltepec's current violence is political. Outsiders covet the mineral and electoral riches in this poor region. So when the surrounding villages' candidate for municipal president, who is from the PRD party, legitimately defeated the PRI party candidate from the municipal center, the PRI decided to impose a new president, and the violence began.

The small line of indigenous pilgrims grew in number that morning as we wound through the village and passed various white stone crosses, where we paused for prayer. The people reflected on their own cultural history of communal sharing and of community and spiritual values. Accumulating and fighting over material things is not a part of the Mixtec culture, one person pointed out. As we gathered at a breathtakingly high point above the village marked by a large stone cross, the many widows and orphans of the violence in the growing crowd one by one voiced heart-wrenching cries for peace.

Late that afternoon, the twelve of us sat by the Río Verde and compared our experiences of the two peace processions in Amoltepec and in the surrounding villages that are part of the municipality. A month later we were still asking ourselves how we could support the cry for peace we heard in that beautiful village.

Word came from leaders in Amoltepec that the pilgrimage was the first statement the community had ever made that peace was possible and that many wanted to continue seeking peace. Though some say the violence "is in our blood, we are warriors," others counter that this is nonsense. Nothing in the Mixtec culture incites to violence. The violence is being provoked for political and economic gain.

Two years later, I ran into a young Mexican religious Sister in the Clínica del Pueblo across the street from our apartment in the city of Oaxaca. At first I didn't recognize her as from Amoltepec. But yes, it turned out that she was one of the four Sisters who invited us to the village years earlier.

"And how are things in Amoltepec?" I asked.

"Worse than ever," she replied, shaking her head. "The political violence has calmed. But now it is over land disputes. One group kidnapped a young man last week, and the rest of the town went on strike demanding his return. He was returned, but dead, with his hands cut off and signs of torture." She sighed, "The children are our only hope — if we can only overcome the culture of revenge!"

The Mixtec culture, it seemed, certainly had its violent side. The strange interchange in the streets of Amoltepec continued to haunt my thoughts:

"It's in our blood. We are warriors!"

"Nonsense! There's nothing in our culture that promotes violence. We are being manipulated from outside."

What was the reality? I had noticed that this type of violence didn't seem to occur in the villages where I worked in the Mixteca Alta. So one day I asked Jesús León, my friend from San Isidro Tilantongo who works with CEDICAM, "Why is it that there is such violence in places like Amoltepec and not here?"

He answered quickly, having obviously thought about this before. "Because our land is so poor that we don't have anything that anyone else wants! No gold, no mineral deposits, no forests."

Quetzalcóatl and the "Reign of Peace"

The question of the reason for the violence of Amoltepec kept bothering me. So I was fascinated when I ran into a couple of books by anthropologists and archeologists telling the story of Quetzalcóatl and the religious and cultural ancestors of the Mixtecs and the other indigenous peoples of Mesoamerica.

According to anthropologist Laurette Séjourné in her book, *El universo de Quetzalcóatl*, beginning in the time of Christ, for almost one thousand years a peaceful and extremely creative society thrived across southern Mexico and Central America. A mystical and contemplative worldview held this culture together. This society believed that the human endeavor consisted in transforming the human and the natural world into a mirror of the holy or the divine.

This vision, in a great outburst of creativity, transformed Mesoamerica into a place of magnificent cities brimming with incredible art and architecture in concentrations perhaps equaled nowhere else in the world of that time. The sites that today have been discovered and excavated bear exotic names: *Tikal, Chichen Itzá, Copán, Monte Albán*. But even more remarkable than this, every fifty-two years these cultures broke down their walls, destroyed murals, and buried their remains to express this culture's belief that, according to Séjourné, life finds its meaning in the transforming of the world and not in its possessing.

The god-king Quetzalcóatl formed the central figure of this civilization. He, like all living beings, struggled to rise above his purely earthly nature and unite with the divine. Through penance and prayer, he achieved enlightenment, becoming pure light, the "Lord of the Dawn."

The principal symbol of Quetzalcóatl in the art of the region, found throughout the remains of the art and literature of the era, was the plumed serpent.

The featherless serpent, also ubiquitous in the stylized *grecas* (abstract geometrical designs whose zigzag form resembles a serpent in motion) found in Mesoamerican temples and pyramids, represents the human species that, like Quetzalcóatl, writhes in motion trying to liberate itself from the purely earthly. Its unity with the divine in enlightenment is represented by the descending eagle, which meets the serpent and metamorphizes into the serpent's feathered form.

A second symbol of Quetzalcóatl in the art of the region was the evening star, Venus. At the end of its 584-day year, as perceived from the earth, Venus disappears from our view for five days until it resurrects with the dawning sun. Quetzalcóatl similarly, in the legend, passes through and overcomes the underworld in a transformative journey to resurrection as the Lord of the Dawn.

Quetzalcóatl was not purely legendary. He lived as a historic king in the city of Tula, and he insisted on peacefulness, specifically prohibited human sacrifice, and taught that only those who passed through spiritual enlightenment were fit to govern the splendid cities of the Mesoamerican jungles.

Séjourné and some other anthropologists suggest that the arrival of more warlike peoples from the north in the ninth and tenth centuries irrevocably changed this peaceful and creative civilization. The nomadic and warlike Aztecs then came to dominate the region. Some believe that from that time on, the Aztec-led culture of war and human sacrifice overcame and submerged the previously peaceful civilizations of the region.

The civilizations that the Spaniards encountered in the late fifteenth century perhaps formed the remnants of a peaceful and artistic society, distorted by the more recent warlike influences. I have heard indigenous spiritual interpreters repeat this same theme of the ultimate peaceful and "civilizing" mission of the original and authentic indigenous cultures, a mission to be carried out for the sake of the planet. And some believed that behind the distortions that have emerged within these cultures and the misrepresentations that Western cultures have given to the indigenous peoples, this mission remains intact today.

Perhaps the ultimate spiritual heritage of the Mixtecs of Amoltepec was, indeed, not the nonsense that they are a people who supposedly had warrior blood, but something deeper and more in tune with what the world was asking of their people in our day.

Violence in Western Culture

What about us? What about those of us who are from this relatively recently born U.S. culture based on strong European roots? If the first Spaniards encountered an indigenous culture already distorted by a new violence and bellicose nature, the Christian European civilization imposed by the Spanish on the region had also departed from the peaceful and high-minded principles of its nominal founder, Jesus, as summarized in the Christian Gospels.

And the violent nature of Western European civilization, and its offshoot, North American civilization, should make us wonder about the origins of this violence, as we do about Mixtec violence, and to what extent it is integral to our culture.[1]

U.S citizens need to hear and know, in a way we can understand and accept, that many ordinary people on the city streets and in the country villages of this world consider the United States to be one of the most violent cultures on the planet today. The raw numbers of wars and killings in which we have been involved give credence to their view. A body count over the last few centuries demonstrates that we, along with our Western European ancestors and relatives, are part of a tradition of violence.

Could it be because it is "in our blood," as some of the Mixtecs of Amoltepec voiced? Or could it be that it is being provoked by something that is not at the root of who we are as citizens of the United States?

The Body Count

It didn't look promising from the start of our U.S civilization. From the arrival of the settlers in Jamestown to 1900, expansion of the first colonies and the eventual conquest of continental U.S. cost, according to Ward Churchill, more than 11 million indigenous lives and dispossessed indigenous peoples of more than 97 percent of their lands.[2] At the same time, our European relatives to the south, according to Bartolomé de Las Casas, exterminated approximately 50 million original inhabitants[3] of what we now call Latin America through war, slavery, and disease.

Polk provoked a war against Mexico in 1848, which not only cost Mexico half of its territories but five thousand lives.[4] U.S. Marine efforts to maintain control in Nicaragua in 1855, 1860, 1909, 1912, and 1926 eliminated 8,525 Nicaraguan lives.[5]

The invasion of the Philippines in 1899–1902 took another 270,000 native lives.[6] In the twentieth century, we and our European brothers combined to kill 15 million people in World War I,[7] and an additional 55 million in World War II.[8] We joined in with a massive elimination of 162,684 Japanese with just two atomic bombs in 1945.[9]

The Korean War claimed 2,367,175 human lives.[10] Then there were the 1,254,748 Vietnamese who had to die.[11]

The invasion of Panama in 1989 cost over 3,000 Panamanian lives.[12] And there was El Salvador, Guatemala, Chile, Granada, and Haiti.

Estimates are that recent U.S. wars in Afghanistan and Iraq have caused 251,102 deaths with 532,715 wounded.[13] U.S. House of Representatives Resolution 333 introduced by Dennis Kucinich states that the Iraqi death toll alone has reached 650,000.[14]

Over the past two centuries the world has paid with millions of bloody deaths for the current North American and European balance of power upon which the present world structure rests. It has indeed been carnage such as the world has never seen, primarily at the hands of the current victors, the United States and the European states.

Once outside the cultural and moral borders of the United States and Western Europe, it becomes reasonable to ask what the real heritage of these Western-dominated centuries has been to the human race. Are the true gifts of the European and American civilizations to this newly globalized world Mozart and Shakespeare, Hemingway and Faulkner, Locke and Jefferson, Rembrandt and the Beatles? Or is the more lasting, pervasive, and effective gift to the world of our civilizations the current violent pattern of economic and military domination that is forcing 3 billion people to live on less than $2 a day?

It was Gandhi who, when asked by a British reporter what he thought of British civilization, said, "I think it would be a good idea." He and his people, on the receiving end of the violence and the externalized costs that kept England's colonial power intact, did not see much difference between British actions and those of Nazi Germany of the time. In our day, we have witnessed our own American soldiers torturing Iraqis, ironically in the very same facility in which Saddam Hussein tortured his victims. While it is very difficult for us, we need to come to terms with the violence we have wrought and continue to perpetrate on the world's citizens, in the name of whatever noble value our country's current leaders invoke in order to numb us to the reality of what we are doing.

Jared Diamond, in *Guns, Germs, and Steel: The Fates of Human Societies,*[15] cites a fascinating array of historical, biological, and cultural "good luck" of the original Europeans to explain the current balance of European and American domination in the world, as Diamond says, *without reference to issues of racial superiority or inferiority*. He argues that European-based domination rested upon an unparalleled and fortuitous variety of domesticable plants and animals, which early Europeans found at their disposal. The scholarship is impressive, and the information overwhelming and convincing from within the confines of the dominant but limited Western cultural worldview. But those outside of the Western cultural and moral boundaries might see the issues differently than Diamond.

First, from outside, it seems that only a European or North American would assume that the current situation of Western domination represents a cultural success rather than a moral failing. And only someone of that background, in our current world, would set out to prove that this "cultural success" is not due to the racial superiority of the peoples of the West. The rest of the world might rather ask, "What kind of people would use the historical favors of nature with which Western Europe was blessed to brutally and violently dominate a colonized world?" To the ordinary people of the non-Western world, who today are scandalized by the TV pictures of Afghan and Iraqi children and families brutalized by U.S. war efforts,[16] deciding to establish this domination involved a moral choice. And they would ask, "What kind of people would make such a choice?"

The Human Nature Excuse

European political philosophers and writers have given us a credible excuse for our cultural behavior. From Thomas Hobbes to Joseph Conrad one strain of European thought has held that the natural state of "man" is war. We are by nature warlike and thus we need structured, if not regimented, societies to avoid the constant insecurity to which this nature would drive us. Present-day neoconservatives mouth similar convictions to defend our aggressive foreign interventions.[17] Life is war, and so we had better join the game — and play to win. Darwin thought that "survival of the fittest" was the basic evolutionary principle of the natural world. We seem to apply that savage principle to human society while marveling at the achievements of our own Western "civilization."

Although from the seats of economic and political power the game may seem like war, in the streets of towns and villages, in indigenous and rural communities, in our own country and around the world, the extreme violence that we see in Amoltepec, as well as in Iraq and Afghanistan, really seems to be the exception rather than the rule. Most of those who philosophized about the violent character of human nature did so and still do so from within a dominant political and economic class. Might this be due to the fact that only by continued violence can these same classes obtain and maintain unjustly gained privileges?

The everyday world of the farmer and worker, of the villager or the city dweller of whatever country, where extreme differences in wealth and poverty do not exist, is much more commonly characterized by cooperative structures and relationships than by violent competition, as much as some might wish to appeal to Darwinian concepts of the "survival of the fittest." Indeed some physicists and biologists are currently suggesting that symbiosis and cooperation are more characteristic of the history of the universe than war and competition.[18]

In any case, any of us who have had friends or relatives return from the wars of our times with deeply scarred and traumatized psyches and spirits, whether they belonged among the winners or the losers of war, would be quick to doubt that this kind of violence is "natural" to the human person. Contradicting what theories about the violence of human nature might suggest, a large number of families of victims of the World Trade Center attacks demonstrated a radically different human reality when they actively and vocally opposed the war of revenge on Afghanistan. Unfortunately, in spite of their opposition, our country invaded both Afghanistan and Iraq in their name and eventually killed many times the number of innocent people who perished in the savage attacks in our own land.

Viewed from the outside, it looks as if North American culture has taken the European mind-set and ideology to its extremes, and there is no easy excuse. We are many things, many of them good. And as individuals we may be very nice. But as a nation we are also a violent people. Over 150 years ago, as President Polk invaded Mexico because Mexico refused to sell all of the present U.S. West to him, Mexican journalist Martinillo wrote of us:

> You can't buy something that the owner doesn't want to sell. You sell it to me or I will kill you is the language of an assailant. It is the language of a bandit, not of a supposedly respectable nation that sings each morning in its schools and churches authentic praises to liberty and presumes that obedience to the law is the sign of civility, and then acts like a barbarian who settles differences with his fists without the least respect for the property of others. The Americans have not evolved in matters of law: they continue to think like Paleolithic man. "I like it. I grab it from you. It's mine. I'm stronger. Shut up!"[19]

But another question still remains, as it does with the people of the Mixteca Alta: Is violence "in our blood," or are the causes of our violence extraneous to who we are?

Latin Americans, who are aware of and often outraged by the historical and present-day violent interventions by the United States in Latin America and around the world, have grown accustomed to excuse the

American people, whom they like and respect, for the excesses of their
political and economic leaders. Contemporary political climates in Argentina, Bolivia, Brazil, and Venezuela as well as Mexico, reveal that this
is beginning to change.

And indeed, if we want to be honest, from a moral standpoint, we
need to ask ourselves if it is just "bad luck" or "fate" that we have
elected an almost unbroken succession of political and foreign policy
leaders who have led us, time and again, into two centuries of wars of
domination, conquest, and economic gain. Is the fact that the U.S. peace
movement must fill the streets of our cities and towns protesting against
one war or another every decade just because we continue to be duped by
aggressive and violent political leaders? Is there some reason why we do
not see that their claims about the necessity of killing massive numbers
of people to assure them democracy, is as hollow as those of the Spanish
Inquisition, which killed its victims to save their souls?

In the words of Mexican journalist Gilberto López y Rivas, "If some
day Bush and his group are judged guilty of crimes against humanity,
will the people of the United States be free of all responsibility?"[20]

Is it in our blood? Or is it perhaps in our ideologies? That is a question
that will take some reflection and some investigation to try to deal with
fairly. But it is a question we must deal with in our time. The present
bellicose behavior of our country is dysfunctional and dangerous for the
human family of the twenty-first century.

Reasons for Amoltepec?

Meanwhile, in a meeting of indigenous campesinos and campesinas, I
ran into a young woman from a village near Amoltepec.

"The violence really began in Amoltepec and our communities when
the government programs to privatize communal lands started in 1996.
Government people armed and paid villagers to assassinate leaders who
were against the privatization efforts," she explained.

A university professor and researcher added, "In Colombia large
mining firms such as Kennecott are involved in provoking violence to
terrorize people into leaving the countryside so such international firms
will be free to exploit rich mineral deposits. Amoltepec and its neighbors
are sitting on top of the largest iron deposits in all of Mexico. We need
to investigate who is behind the killings."

And who or what is behind the centuries of bloodletting that has
characterized European and U.S. history?

In the past four chapters we have seen strengths and weaknesses in our own cultural values and in those of the indigenous Mixtec. How can this experience help us in a twenty-first-century world that is so much at war and balancing precariously between sustainability and disaster? Hope emerges from unexpected places. Outside the borders of our cultural and moral limitations, in Latin America and across the Global South, alternative ways of living together and living with our planet are beginning to take shape, often based on indigenous insights. They may at first seem "alien" to our ways of thinking. But as they make their way across our cultural and moral borders, as we will see in the following chapters, they may offer us a new hope for a different kind of twenty-first century.

Interlude

When we invited you on this journey into the villages of the Mixteca Alta, leaving behind some of the values and ways of thinking that we are accustomed to on that side of the U.S. border, we hoped to share with you a cultural adventure like the one we have lived among Mixtec campesinos. We also hoped that it would help make the world bigger, richer, and more exciting for you, as it has for us.

We have learned through our experience that the Mixtec people live out some very different ideas about wealth and poverty, about the community and the individual, about property and family, about the natural world, as well as about work and about happiness. Yet, they are also susceptible to some of the distortions and manipulations that have led us, principally in the United States but also in Europe, to a century of killing at levels never before seen in human history.

In the process of our journey, we have also seen that our own European-based culture, though containing many positive traits, has some engrained values and presuppositions that put us, our ways of living, to say nothing of the planet where we live, at serious risk for survival in this twenty-first century. Many of these values and presuppositions have become almost articles of faith for our culture. Sometimes we refer to this collection of values as the "real world." Those who don't subscribe to these ideas have, we tend to think, not joined the "real world." The "articles of faith" look something like this:

- Life is about getting a good job so as to have the things we want in life.
- A sound economy demands continuous growth.
- Economic growth creates wealth.
- The resources of the world are for those who can take them and develop them.

- The American Way of Life is the model for successful countries and societies in this world.

- The United States is politically and economically dominant in this world because of its superior organization, work ethic, and moral values.

- Competition for the world's resources should be open and unfettered by government interference.

- Other people are poor because they don't have the skills and know-how that we have.

- Most people in the world want to have what we have and to be like us.

- Private property is an earned right.

- Science and technology will find ways for us to all have what we want in the future.

- The natural world and its resources exist primarily for the use of human beings.

As we saw, the Mixtec people would disagree with us on every one of these modern articles of faith. Their "articles of faith" might look something like this:

- The point of life is to live harmoniously in community.

- The planet and all its beings are living relations of ours, gifts of our Mother Earth, and are to be respected as neighbors.

- The other species of the earth are for our use when we need them, but we need to use them with respect.

- Asking permission of Mother Earth and its other creatures and giving thanks for the bounty they provide are essential human practices.

- The goods of the earth are limited, and therefore if one person or species takes too much of those goods, some will be left without enough.

- Individual possessions are not things to hoard but to use for the family and to share with the community.

- Political position is to be used to serve the community and create harmony.

- Fiesta and celebration are an essential part of human community.

We saw that there is strong reason to believe that the natural environment of the planet earth cannot sustain global societies built upon the first set of values and presuppositions, the one we sometimes call the "real world." The planet's resource base and natural systems would have to be duplicated many times for it to support a lifestyle based on the above values extended globally.

Finally, we saw that nearly 3 billion people, or about half the world's population, live in the shadow of ghettos of wealth in the North. They witness these wealthy ghettos daily through their television screens while they live on less than two dollars a day. And we have seen that this is not socially sustainable.

In fundamental ways our current direction creates scarcity, not wealth, increased poverty, not well-being, and endangers the human experiment on this earth.

Our "articles of faith" do not so much represent the way the world is as they represent the rules and the rationale for one way to play the game of living on this planet. In its fundamental outlines, the Mixtec culture represents one of a number of alternative games that have been played successfully by our human community throughout its history.

The good news is that a world based upon our articles of faith is not the only option for our future. The world as it has been explained to us is not the one and only "real world." In fact, peoples like the Mixtecs have envisioned and have successfully lived in a very different way for thousands of years.

Today, indigenous peoples, workers, marginalized people, and campesinos around Latin America and the larger world have undertaken to revise this world in crisis from outside the articles of faith that we have developed in the West. We have a choice. We can defensively and violently hold onto the beliefs and values, the rules and games that threaten the planet and our human society. Or we can begin to take seriously the proposals coming from indigenous peoples and the grassroots Global South for some keys to other, more viable ways to approach our planet and its human and natural life community.

Part III

Learning Hope

Chapter Eight

Mary's Paradox

U.S. Policy Errors Stimulate
New Visions in the Global South

A Vision from Below

Aaron Santiago stood on the mountainside. Below him and us stretched the rugged landscape of the villages of Tilantongo in this isolated region of Oaxaca. Looking down at the eroded, rocky hillsides, I could now see that they were girded with row upon row of contour ditches. Aaron and the Mixtec people had revived a millennia-old indigenous technology for holding soils in place and catching rain water to refill thirsty aquifers on steep mountainsides.

He told us to look more closely, and then we began to distinguish them. Stretching across the seeming barren rocks and *arroyos,* we could see a light green blanket of tens of thousands of newly planted native trees.

"In the past five years we have planted over a million tree seedlings in these villages," he explained. "We don't do this just for our children, nor even for our grandchildren. We do it because the world needs it."

Aaron is a campesino promoter for the Center for Integral Campesino Development of the Mixteca, CEDICAM, in one of the poorest and most eroded areas of southern Mexico. This means he leaves his fields many hours of each month and goes in a team with another promoter to teach other villages about reforestation, rain water catchment, and healthy ways to farm that incorporate new and ancient methods he and his companions have found successful on their own small plots of land.

Their work is profound and inspiring. They have transformed hundreds of acres of barren land that no longer produced decent crops into

Aaron Santiago with newly terraced and reforested hillsides in the background

new forests and richly productive *milpas* where they interplant corn, beans, and squash. But Aaron's words are also profound. They express something that is being heard in many areas of Latin America: a new recognition that the cause of the poor, the cause of the environment, and the cause of the powerless are coming together as never before in our times.

When Aaron links the needs of his people to the needs of the environment and the planet, he reflects a vision of indigenous and campesino communities from Chile to Brazil, and from Ecuador to southern Mexico. These communities are recognizing that their future, that their prosperity on the land does not depend on the next technological innovation that will be imported from the North. It depends, instead, on caring for their local environment, for the Mother Earth whom they have respected for millennia.

They are recognizing that the powerful of this planet, those who set the political agendas of this globalized world, have created economic systems and production systems that the planetary environment cannot sustain. In their rush toward economic domination and short-term profits, the powerful have become blinded to the fact that they are putting the human endeavor on this planet in danger of failure and extinction.

Indigenous communities are seeing that indigenous visions of an interdependent world of great biodiversity and calling for respect among the life species forms a more practical and also a more noble world vision than that of those who currently have the power.

And these, the "powerless" ones of the world, are, along with Aaron, offering us an alternative future. Aaron and CEDICAM say with every tree they plant, "This planet has a future!" With their contour ditches they are recharging the aquifers on whose sweet water we all ultimately depend. With natural fertilizers and green manure crops they are rebuilding the soils on which all life depends. They defend the biodiversity of hundreds of varieties of ancient and richly diverse corn seeds from the onslaught of genetically modified species so that we will all have the gene pools we will need for the future. They create and sustain real wealth.

They are joined by indigenous communities of Bolivia, the Mapuches of Argentina and Chile, the landless campesinos of Brazil, and the movements against the privatization of the basic resources of the planet, a great human movement from below. Instead of an environmentally suicidal culture of greed, instead of the threat of endless "resource wars," they offer a vision of a peace based on an intelligent conservation and a far-sighted sharing of the limited resources of this jewel of a planet.

Mary's Paradox

Paradoxically, U.S. political and economic policy is partly responsible for stimulating these new visions in the South.

Kathy and I were back in the United States for a few weeks giving a talk at our alma mater, Carleton College, in Northfield, Minnesota, visiting friends, and getting together with our children. We had a great time at Carleton, where, after a forty-year absence, we were very impressed with how concerned and involved our classmates have been over the years trying to build a peaceful and environmentally sound future for our children and grandchildren.

Yet, being there made one very aware of the contrasts between life in southern Mexico and in the United States. One friend reading our newsletter wrote back saying our experience in Mexico seemed so different and remote that it was hard to relate to it. We could understand that feeling more from there within the confines of U.S. culture, where we, too, felt cushioned from outside information and points of view and isolated by filtered media coverage.

But let's look at an American story of one family, friends of many years, that we visited on our way back from Minnesota to New Mexico, because their experience makes the connections between realities lived in southern Mexico and there in the United States so clear.

Mary and Virgil farmed organic vegetables with us in Wisconsin in the 1970s when we lived in community together. Several years later, they returned to Nebraska to continue the family farm belonging to Virgil's folks. Recently, they were forced to quit farming due to a number of factors, including decades of U.S. farm policy that has favored large agribusiness companies at the expense of family farms. Fortunately, Virgil and Mary were able to find good jobs in town so they could continue to raise their family in rural Nebraska.

A few weeks before our semi-annual trip home to the United States, to visit our children, we received a letter from Mary. "I need to know more about the effects of NAFTA there in Mexico," she wrote. She then explained how the electronics factory where she had been working had just that week announced it was moving operations to Mexico. "Yet," she continued, "when I went to the unemployment office to put in my application for work elsewhere, there was a long line of Mexican workers in line ahead of me."

Mary's experience highlights the twin paradoxes of U.S firms moving to Mexico while Mexican workers are moving to the United States, and of small U.S. farmers going out of business while U.S. exports of basic grains increase dramatically. But the paradoxical nature of these facts disappears when we realize that both phenomena have a common cause: U.S. economic and trade policies designed by and for transnational corporations pursuing the singular and narrow interest of their shareholders—to make money.

The 1996 U.S. Farm Bill threw farm prices to the mercy of the "market," not a market guided by the proverbial "invisible hand," but rather by monopolizing conglomerates whose economic power was so vast as to be able to create commodity prices so low they didn't cover farmers' production costs. The resulting low market prices for basic grains, which continue to force U.S. small farmers off the land, had to be supplemented with huge U.S. government subsidies to keep the farm sector from collapse. When combined with export subsidies to large grain and agricultural seed and fertilizer companies and free trade agreements under NAFTA that reduce or eliminate Mexican tariffs on almost all U.S. agricultural products, these forces allow sale of U.S. grains at 20 percent to 40 percent below the cost of production in Mexico. This technically illegal dumping by the United States has killed regional, local, and national markets for Mexican campesino farmers and driven an estimated 15 million rural Mexicans off the land since NAFTA was signed in 1994.

Not surprisingly, in spite of tight border patrolling and deadly border deserts that have killed thousands of these rural migrants since 1994, many have arrived in places like Nebraska. Mexicans estimate that another 590,000 people will be forced from rural Mexico in 2008 alone, by the elimination of more tariffs and barriers to U.S. products as a result of NAFTA.[1]

But foreign investment in Mexican industry was supposed to create the jobs to offset such dislocations. Mexican and U.S. politicians especially put their hopes and the hopes of the Mexican nation on foreign assembly plants, or *maquiladoras*. Under NAFTA, parts manufactured in the U.S. would be assembled in these plants by low-wage Mexican workers, and the finished product shipped again duty free for sale in the original developed country.

The forty to eighty cents an hour wages in these plants is the reason why Mary's plant in Nebraska is moving to Mexico. Such wages, however, do not create the kind of Mexican consumers that can stimulate Mexico's economy, nor do they do much to slow the flow of displaced farmers north. Now, to make matters worse for Mexicans (since forty cents an hour is, if you are desperate enough, better than nothing), many assembly plants are moving out of Mexico because they have discovered places where they can pay even lower wages in Central America and China.

Clearly this type of economic and agricultural policy, and the free trade agreements that accompany it, hurt Mexican and U.S. small farmers and workers equally. Small world! No matter how different are our technologies and our lifestyles, we are in this together now in this globalized world.[2] Mary's paradox is not so paradoxical after all.

When we returned to Mexico from the United States, I was quickly off on a trip to Honduras with Mexican campesino representatives for organizing work against the economic models that are creating Mary's paradox. There it became clear that farmers, workers, and the poor from this part of the Global South and in the U.S. are being stimulated by these impossible policies to join together to insist that such models are not inevitable, and do not serve the greater good of the United States or the developing world. And these same campesinos are beginning to demand and build alternatives. Underlying these alternatives is reasoning similar to that of Aaron Santiago: we build new visions "because the world needs it."

The Paradox of Hope

Companies such as Monsanto continue to join with their allies in the U.S. government and with local elites in developing countries to create an unworkable dependence of farmers around the world on their genetically modified seeds and their chemical agricultural products. The 1996 Farm Bill throws prices and agricultural production levels to the wind of a "free market" dominated by monopoly conglomerates. And U.S. political leaders from the current administration continue to prepare us for the endless wars that maintaining this kind of domination of the world's resources will require.

Joseph Stiglitz, in *Globalization and Its Discontents,* debunks the claim that such economic behavior is a recipe for development. The development that did take place with the so-called "Asian tigers" was based on a very different kind of economic globalization where countries receiving foreign investment and foreign industries insisted upon fair wages and treatment for workers, use of local inputs, and transfer of technologies to the host countries, three elements conspicuously absent in NAFTA and in the current model of economic "liberalization" and free trade.

Yet in what seems a paradoxical development it is precisely this current model and its excesses that are contributing to a new hope in Latin America. Indigenous communities, workers, and campesinos are being stimulated to think through alternative models to face the deep poverty that "liberal" economics and U.S. domination have helped to create. Recently the newly elected indigenous president of Bolivia, Evo Morales, proclaimed, "We, the indigenous and original peoples of the world, are the moral reserve of humanity." Could the alternatives that such people are creating represent a hope for us as well? Is there a viable alternative developing?

The other day I drove up into the mountains above the valley of Nochixtlán to deliver a message to Aaron's village where there is only one phone and it is usually inoperative. As I wound up the mountainside over the rocks and ruts, the villages below shrank in my eyesight to tiny grids of brown dirt paths and minuscule houses. I was looking for Jesús Santiago and his brother, Atanacio, two of Aaron's boys, to give them a message about a meeting of Niño a Niño, the organization my wife, Kathy, works with. I cleared the summit and followed the dirt strip that clung to the ridge-top amid dwarf oak stands. As I got closer to El Progreso, my destination, the mountainsides once again went bare and treeless. Finally I cleared that last rise and found myself looking down on the valley of El Progreso.

I hadn't been in this valley so dear to Aaron for a few months, and I was stunned by the green valley and hillsides that lay before me. Where once there had been only barren, rocky, white-soiled landscape, the green of thousands of trees that were planted last year was already taking over. As I wound around the mountainside toward the home of the two boys and their father, the trees from each previous year's plantings I passed were taller, and every mountainside was covered with contour ditches to catch rain water, feeding the thirsty roots of the trees and penetrating to aquifers below.

When I arrived at the tiny one-room cement-block house, it was Atanacio who came running out. No one else was home, so the sixteen-year-old proudly took me on a tour of the nurseries where they were sprouting tens of thousands of native pine and oak. He pointed out complete hillsides of new contour ditches protecting previously barren soils. He explained how the ditches had filled many times that summer with the good rains that fell. His enthusiasm for the work the family and community had accomplished radiated from his smiling face.

"And we can see the volcano from here!" he announced. "There are not many places where you can say that you can see a volcano."

"What, Popocatepetl?" I asked, surprised.

"No. The other . . . uh, Orizaba." He beckoned me to the top of the hill just above the tree nursery. There on the horizon, like a small white cloud in the cloudless blue sky rose the white, snow-covered cone of the volcano Orizaba, shimmering in the faraway Veracruz sunlight.

Not only Atanacio but this whole indigenous valley of El Progreso exuded hope. Hope for rescuing this mountain environment from ecological disaster, hope for indigenous communities and cultures, hope for young people who might not have to leave their valleys and migrate to strange and faraway places in search of economic survival. I thought about the village children with whom he and his older brother, Jesús, worked.

"The village kids are lucky to have you two who love the land so much to help them learn that there are alternatives to migration right here in El Progreso," I mused out loud.

As I drove back down the mountainside, I pondered how the indigenous people of Oaxaca and many other places from Asia to Africa and across Latin America represent a hope, not just for themselves and their own villages and communities, but for us all.

It is no longer possible to pretend that we live in a world of inexhaustible wealth, ecologically or economically, where unending growth is an option. The typical way out of this dilemma for people who find themselves on the top, economically and in terms of access to resources, is to blame population growth. The indigenous thinkers of today recognize that the problem is much deeper than this and counsel us to work for a more sustainable and equitable distribution of the limited goods of the planet. Hidden away in the distant past of Western civilization's Jewish/Christian ideology is a similar call to a just sharing of creation's gifts. Could we re-discover this ancient and contemporary tradition in our own culture with the help of the indigenous peoples today? In a Western world where, for many, hope itself clings to life by a thread, could the indigenous people indeed represent a moral reserve for humanity?

Chapter Nine

The Organizing Poor and Their Advocates

Values for a Hopeful Planet

What can the indigenous movements of the Global South, the campesino communities of Mexico and Latin America, possibly have to teach us?

In the fall of 2005, a small group of women from the village of San Dionisio Ocotepec came together to found a community-based pharmacy. Ten thousand Zapotec people, neighbors of the Mixtecs, inhabit San Dionisio.

Several of these women participated in a workshop offered by Services for an Alternative Education (Servicios para una Educación Alternativa, EDUCA), a not-for-profit Oaxaca City-based organization dedicated to the support and development of indigenous peoples. Their imagination stimulated, this small group of women, short in stature, tall in vision, noted that San Dionisio had no access to a reliable pharmacy. Its families had to travel a half day, round-trip, and pay roughly half a day's wage to purchase medicines.

Lidia, one of the pharmacy's organizers explained one day, "It's really more than a pharmacy. We're really concerned about the health of our town. We see ourselves as health promoters." To that end the Committee, as they call themselves, made contact with two established health organizations to request additional training. Within a couple of months, they had arranged for ongoing training with the Clinic of the People (La Clínica del Pueblo), dedicated to Western medicine, and with PROSA (Promotores de Salud), another grassroots group that specializes in indigenous medical practices.

At one meeting I attended, the five women present all chimed in enthusiastically and simultaneously to emphasize their commitment to recover

Memorial to Korean farmer Hung Lee, who immolated himself during demonstrations against the World Trade Organization in Cancún, Mexico, in 2003

the indigenous medical practices that they see disappearing. One woman, Magda, pointed out, "Our traditional ways are less expensive and many of them work better than the Western medicines that the local clinic doctor tells us we need to buy." Julieta at this point commented, "And it's not just about our traditional practices. It also has to do with our language. We're losing our language, too. Several years ago, we confronted the village teachers sent here from other states when we found out they were punishing our children for speaking Zapotec in school."

The name that the Committee chose for the community pharmacy inspires. I enjoyed the privilege of participating in the moment when they named their pharmacy "Yedaan." Yedaan is Zapotec for a plant that translates to the "Tree of Life." Indigenous healers use Yedaan to prepare a warm herbal bath for women who have just given birth. Yedaan helps them to recover and be fully revitalized. But Yedaan's meaning goes deeper. In the Zapotec dialect spoken in San Dionisio, in reply to the question, "How are you?" one would reply "Yedaan" to indicate that all is well with you and your family as well. I was delighted with the name they chose.

These women care about their community, and they identified a specific service they could provide. Profit did not motivate them; they have set up their project as a nonprofit organization and each will volunteer her time to operate it. Service motivates them. They are determined, hard-working, and persistent. They link health needs with the desire to maintain their Zapotec way of life. Realistic and practical, they are combining the best of Western medicine and traditional medicine in their health promotion work — and perhaps the best of two visions of culture.

Citizens' Movements:
The World's Second Superpower

The spirit of *Yedaan*, the Tree of Life, offers hope not only to San Dionisio, but to the whole world. It is a spirit we are finding among indigenous people across the hemisphere. It is a spirit of service, of solidarity, of caring and generosity, of community. But it is also a spirit that is global. It tends to express itself in Aaron's words. "The world needs us" to work with this spirit. This spirit, wherever it may be found, does indeed represent a moral reserve for humanity and a hope for our twenty-first century. In Oaxaca, *Yedaan* forms one small example of a movement comprising perhaps millions of similar projects around the globe. Some have referred to these movements in the collective as the world's "second superpower."[1]

"Civil society" is another term used throughout Latin America for this "second world superpower." It is made up of unions, not-for-profit organizations, student and indigenous groups, religious and human rights organizations, all falling outside the strictly governmental and business spheres of society. Civil society has a history in Latin America of being a force for change — recently toppling governments in Ecuador, Argentina, and Bolivia. Counterparts in the United States would include the civil rights movements, the anti-war movement, and the current "anti-globalization" movement, and the sustainable community movement.

The good news for us is that, at the present, the movements for change that are growing in the United States are mirrored by energetic groups from the Global South who with great conviction and creativity are promoting an alternative future for our planet. And it may be this great energy from the South that will tip the scales in favor of a rational future in the coming decades. It is an energy we don't often hear about in our U.S. media, but it is one that should give us hope.

Hope for Local Communities, Hope for Us

Throughout Latin America new groups are forming around a fresh vision of an inclusive democracy, more egalitarian economies, and a new respect for the indigenous environmental worldview. La Alianza, in Barquisimeto, Venezuela, is one such group. Some thirty years ago the people of this medium-sized city in northern Venezuela, with the help of a committed religious group from France called the Little Brothers of Jesus, founded La Alianza. Today it supports small farmers who produce organic products and helps farmers develop markets for their harvests. It also supports a bread-baking cooperative. And it cooperates with training and education programs in the poorest neighborhoods of Barquisimeto along with a collective of private schools called Fe y Alegría (faith and joy).

There are groups throughout Latin America that represent this spirit of global solidarity and service. In war-torn Colombia, Movimiento Continental por los Cristianos por la Paz con Justicia y Dignidad (Continental Movement of Christians for Peace with Justice and Dignity) represents another example of this spirit of hope and solidarity: highly dedicated individuals working from a Christian religious motivation. Founded in 2004, by a small representation of religiously motivated justice and service workers, Movimiento Continental por los Cristianos por la Paz con Justicia y Dignidad,[2] supports and reconnects those attempting to work for social and economic change across the Americas. This organization, though still young, includes participants from Guatemala, Mexico, Colombia, Brazil, Argentina, Canada, France, the United States, and Venezuela.

The spirit that motivates this other way of playing the economic and social game in our time is found not only in Latin America. OneWorld Radio in Lusaka, Zambia, is part of the hope. You can find OneWorld Radio on the web at *www.radio.oneworld.net*. It connects some one thousand members from eighty-three countries by providing audio programs in common MP3 or Real Audio formats. OneWorld Radio makes sure people's voices are heard by providing free access to audio material from all over the world. Members of OneWorld promote social justice, they form part of an international community demanding human rights, and they work for sustainable development to end poverty.

OneWorld Radio is affiliated with *OneWorld.net* based in the UK. Anyone with access to the Internet from South Africa to the rural Mixteca can listen to audio programs in major languages classified in no fewer than ninety-seven topic areas. For example, OneWorld Radio daily offers up to 67 programs on climate change, 229 on civil society, and 32 on refugees.

Our African partners through OneWorld have pulled up a chair to the roundtable to build a different future.

And there is hope that even governments can learn to play the game differently, with the spirit of *Yedaan.*

In January 2006, fellow missioner and co-author Steve Hicken visited a textile cooperative in Caracas, Venezuela, made up of 199 women. He writes:

> As I entered the large, well illuminated, airy and spacious building where some one hundred women were working, the first thing that I noticed was how cheerful they all were. Some women were working alone, some in groups, some were coordinating tasks, some simply chatted. As we entered, I spotted a longtime friend, Carmen, whose face lit up as she left her workspace and walked over to greet me.
>
> During the next two hours I became acquainted with the Núcleo Endógeno Fabricio Ojeda. *Endogeno* doesn't translate well into the English "endogenous," but the meaning is along the lines of "homegrown," "indigenous," "from our own backyard." Fabricio Ojeda was a Venezuelan political leader active in the 1960s. *Núcleo,* is nucleus, or center.
>
> The textile cooperative constitutes only one part of the center, which also includes a medical clinic, a shoe manufacturing cooperative, an agricultural center innovating forms of cultivation appropriate in urban environments, and three large, illuminated basketball courts complete with nets attached to the rims (a rarity in much of Latin America).
>
> I mused how ironic it was that the Núcleo Endógeno Fabricio Ojeda was constructed on the site of an abandoned facility formerly operated by Venezuela's national oil company, PDVSA. It is located in one of the poorest zones at the western end of Caracas, in Gramoven.
>
> Over the next few days, I learned that the governments, too, may play a constructive role in supporting the organization of civil society. The Venezuelan government has created a department which it calls the Ministry of Popular Economics, and this department initiated the center which I visited in Gramoven. The department

exists to channel public resources toward creating and supporting citizen-led economic initiatives. Members of the shoe and textile cooperatives at Núcleo Endógeno Fabricio Ojeda emphasized that members themselves have created and support their management structure, and the cooperative belongs to all the members. They also explained that the Ministry of Popular Economics had opened the space for them and provided the manufacturing equipment and initial training.

The Venezuelan Ministry of Popular Economics (Ministerio para la Economía Popular, MINEP) aims to strengthen, consolidate, and expand economic participation and productivity of the impoverished of Venezuela in order to help them to improve the quality of their lives. Toward this end MINEP has created 130 centers similar to the Núcleo Endógeno Fabricio Ojeda around the country. Aside from the Núcleos Endógenos, MINEP has founded and now manages the Development Bank for Women and the Bank of the People, both institutions offering micro loans for small economic projects.[3] MINEP includes a training institute, the Instituto Nacional de Cooperación Educativa, as well as several donation and grant-making institutes. In this way the Venezuelan government channels income from oil exports to building grassroots citizens' organizations.

The World Social Forum

One organization with a global reach, the World Social Forum (WSF),[4] attempts to connect the hope represented by the world's growing civil society movements.

On January 25, 2001, approximately twenty thousand people met in Porto Alegre Brazil for the first World Social Forum. Since then the Social Forum has expanded from a single event to a permanent coordinating body sponsoring annual conferences. The growth of attendance at World Social Forums has been impressive. According to the statistics the WSF keeps, participation levels grew rapidly.

2001 — Porto Alegre, Brazil: 20,000

2002 — Porto Alegre, Brazil: 50,000

2003 — Porto Alegre, Brazil: 100,000

2004 — Mumbai, India: 115,000

2005 — Porto Alegre, Brazil: 155,000

2006 — Multiple locations: Caracas, Venezuela, 50,000; Karachi, Pakistan; and Bamako, Mali. Attendance estimates for Pakistan and Mali unavailable at this writing.[5]

The World Social forum describes itself as:

> an open meeting place where social movements, networks, NGOs and other civil society organizations opposed to neo-liberalism and a world dominated by capital or by any form of imperialism come together to pursue their thinking, to debate ideas democratically, to formulate proposals, share their experiences freely, and network for effective action. Since the first world encounter in 2001, it has taken the form of a permanent world process seeking and building alternatives to neo-liberal policies. This definition is in its Charter of Principles, the WSF's guiding document.
>
> The World Social Forum is also characterized by plurality and diversity, is non-confessional, non-governmental, and non-partisan. It proposes to facilitate decentralized coordination and networking among organizations engaged in concrete action toward building another world, at any level from the local to the international, but it does not intend to be a body representing world civil society. The World Social Forum is not a group or an organization.[6]

The founding slogan of the World Social Forum reads, hopefully: "Another World Is Possible."

Steve continues his account of his visit to Venezuela saying: "I attended the World Social Forum in Caracas, Venezuela. There I joined some 50,000 other participants looking to exchange ideas as to why we thought we needed a different world in the first place, what that other world might look like and how we might get from this world to that 'other' one. The World Social Forum has contributed enormously to organizing, imagining, and also engineering the changes this present book points us toward."

Civil Society and Change

The other day Jesús León and I were discussing the vigorous protests of the teachers union here in Oaxaca, which succeeded in breaking the power of the dominant political party in the state (the PRI) in recent elections, and which is threatening to unseat a corrupt governor. "You in the United States are so timid," he commented in response to my surprise at the tenacity and combativeness of the men and women of the teachers union. And indeed we do underestimate the power of civil society organizing.

It was only through such organizing that India achieved its independence from the British Empire, that South Africa freed itself from apartheid, that African Americans achieved significant social gains during the civil rights movement. Civil society organizing ended the Vietnam War, began the environmental movement, and through it women have made significant progress in the last decades toward gender equity in the United States and Europe. Governments didn't initiate these changes, nor did private enterprise. What these movements of committed individuals and organized groups achieved are some of the most striking and life-affirming changes of the last century. And they achieved these enormous changes almost exclusively through nonviolent means.

Much as the above examples indicate, the world's citizens' movements have awakened in our times and we need to feel the hope that this promises. The leadership may most likely come from the Global South since that is where the greatest excesses of the current economic and social models are felt and where, as a result, new creative energy is being stimulated. The people of the South are also free of the assumptions we have in the North about the inevitability of the world as it is presently arranged — assumptions that cripple not only our hope but our imagination and our vital energy.[7]

Global Hope from Campesino and Indigenous Communities in the South

Not only Mixtec farmers but also campesino communities across Latin America exemplify this spirit, as I was to discover in Managua, Nicaragua, a few years ago.

Dozens of men, women, and children sold water, candies, and auto parts at each busy street corner as I arrived at the National University of Engineering in Managua, Nicaragua, for the second Encuentro Campesino, a meeting of small farmers from across Mesoamerica. I had passed children and young people begging for money for food outside the parking lots of U.S.-style shopping centers. On my way from Mexico across Central America I had heard in country after country the same story of growing collapse of rural economies and catastrophic unemployment.

But let me back up a bit and tell you why I was at the university in Managua.

Soon after we arrived in Mexico and I began work with Mexican indigenous campesino groups, it began to be clear to me that the 80 percent poverty rate in the Mexican countryside was not primarily due to ignorance, poor soils, or antiquated technologies. Though most of us North Americans would like to believe that poverty can be overcome in the rest of the world through better technologies and a greater imitation of our American work ethic and lifestyle — with some intelligent charity thrown in by us from "the North" — a more complicated reality quickly forced itself upon me.

People in the Mexican countryside of Oaxaca are poorer than ever because the market now pays them almost nothing for their crops. Many are desperately in debt because their "intelligent" investment in updated farming technologies (which promised to allow them to compete in an international market) has run up against a manipulated market that has double-crossed them with prices below their cost of production. The price of corn, for instance, is determined by the three U.S. conglomerates that control 82 percent of U.S. corn exports, Cargill, Archer Daniels Midland, and Zen Noh.[8] Even the very "modern" agricultural technologies highly dependent on chemical pesticides, fertilizers, mechanization, irrigated land, and hybrid seeds that we are accustomed to think are the solution to poverty have contributed to the degradation of their soils, a degeneration in their health, and are in any case, no longer affordable to them.[9]

These newly discovered realities led me to follow large and ever growing popular international forums, organized by campesino and indigenous movements and NGOs. First I followed them to Tapachula, Mexico, then to Quetzaltenango, Guatemala, and now to Managua. Why is poverty growing in Latin America? Why is the gap between rich and poor increasing? And what are the alternatives?

In Managua, Nicaragua, that July of 2002, the international forum was taking place inside the national university. There as I listened to campesinos explain, I continued to try to get it clear. Campesino and indigenous leaders from forty-five organizations of Mexico and Central America had met there to protest the trade agreements and the economic model that they hold responsible for the growing desperation — and to propose alternatives. They are part of what is quickly evolving into a broad-based and militant movement of social sectors across

Mesoamerica that says it is in a "war of economic models" against the current version of free trade and globalization.[10]

At the same time that we were meeting with over one thousand delegates from over three hundred campesino and indigenous organizations, on the other side of Managua the Nicaraguan national organization of *maquiladora* workers and the organization of banana workers met to denounce the newest megaplan for the area, the "Plan Puebla Panama," and the expansion of its development model across Latin America under the Free Trade Area of the Americas (FTAA). They were responding to what they described as a "worldwide war instigated by the powerful countries and transnational corporations to dismantle the agriculture of small nations and eliminate the campesino or small subsistence farm economy that has sustained indigenous and rural communities for millennia."[11]

We have already seen how new waves of migration from Mexico are related to free trade. And farmers from Costa Rica, Panama, Guatemala, El Salvador, Honduras, and Nicaragua were telling a similar story.

How do free trade agreements damage local economies in developing countries?

1. By subsidizing northern agribusiness production while forcing developing countries to eliminate subsidies to their agricultural sectors. The 1996 U.S. Farm Bill provided $57 billion of subsidies to U.S. producers over ten years with 70 percent going to the largest 10 percent of the agro-industrial producers.

2. By forcing small countries, in the name of free trade, to open their domestic markets to U.S. imports duty free.

3. By the dumping of basic grains on Mexican and other markets by U.S. agribusiness companies, aided by the above subsidies. According to Tina Rosenberg in the *New York Times*,[12] U.S. agribusiness firms are dumping at 20 percent below the cost of production. As a result, corn today brings the Mexican campesino less than 50 percent of what it did a few years ago. The story is similar with pineapple, coffee, and sugar cane. Of course, the campesino economy is collapsing.

Once having "proved," using these asymmetrical trade agreements, that campesino agricultural production is "inefficient and unsustainable," those benefiting from this brand of monopoly capitalism, which is anything but "free trade," can proceed to justify creating dependence of small countries on northern agribusiness for their food needs and can pressure developing countries to turn over rural resources to international private investors who will create plantation farms, mines, and hydroelectric projects to "efficiently" exploit them for private gain.[13] In places like Oaxaca, Mexico, 80 percent of the land is still held communally by indigenous campesinos who form an unwanted obstacle to such private investment.

In two days of intense work, the forum of campesinos in Managua rejected the idea that an agricultural economy that requires $57 billion in subsidies is more competitive than campesino production. "Though small producers do not have the same *economic* yields as the large producers," they observed, "they are much more efficient in the generation of employment, of just incomes, in the production of total food, and in producing food security, as well as in the preservation and reproduction of natural resources and biodiversity."[14] Recent studies by the U.S. nongovernmental organization Food First seem to support their observations. Food First found small, diversified producers generated from 200 to 1000 percent more total food per acre than large agribusiness farmers.[15]

But paradoxically the very trade agreements and economic models that the campesinos in Managua felt were so damaging to their livelihoods were also stimulating them to visions of hopeful alternatives. At the end of the meeting campesinos committed themselves to rebuild campesino economies, forging new links to consumers and promoting alternative agricultural techniques such as organic farming which will be freer of market forces with production targeted for local instead of international markets. They encouraged the promotion and protection of traditional native seeds of indigenous and campesino communities in the face of transgenic and hybrid seeds from northern agribusinesses that seek to create a market dependence. And they pledged themselves to the formation of a "popular economy" among poor producers and consumers focused on production for basic needs, barter and non-money exchanges, and joining with "fair trade" groups in the North. I had heard these same themes emerging among Mexican campesinos, and I felt encouraged hearing these positive proposals from this group of campesinos from across Central America.

Having watched the free trade model collapse in Argentina, while political leaders running on anti–free trade tickets have won elections in Brazil, Bolivia, Uruguay, Venezuela, and Ecuador, both the militancy and the hope of campesinos and workers is growing across the Americas. And, as in Managua, they are forming into a new power with which to be reckoned. Typical of the spirit of these new movements are the principles that came out of a similar conference in Tapachula, Mexico. They proclaim a perceptive vision. It is a vision reminiscent of *Yedaan* and the village of San Dionisio Ocotepec, of Aaron Santiago of El Progreso Tilantongo and the 1 million trees planted because the world needs them:

- The earth and water, the forests, biodiversity, agricultural knowledge, traditional medicine, and the indigenous culture are communal goods, part of the common patrimony of human beings and *are not merchandise!* Therefore, agriculture should be excluded from the activities of the World Trade Organization, from the Free Trade Area of Americas, if it should pass, and the agricultural agreements of NAFTA need to be revised.

- Privatizations, sacking of natural resources, and environmentally aggressive technologies are driving us toward a social and environmental catastrophe of planetary proportions. In the face of this, we need a campesino agriculture that is economically viable, socially just, and environmentally healthy.

- The poor countries must regain food sovereignty, since the empire [referring to the United States and international financial institutions] is using food as a weapon. Strong campesino agriculture with the support of public policies can stem the tide of emigration, with an emphasis on production for local and national, not just international markets.[16]

These visionary words of the indigenous peoples and campesinos of Mesoamerica remind us of the other groups we have mentioned organizing themselves in Latin America. And the people who are organizing around these ideas and visions, when joined with the international social movements in Asia, Africa, Europe, and the United States, do indeed represent a "second world superpower."

They represent not only political and economic alternatives, but a different hope for the twenty-first century. While Western leaders are talking about the a future of trade and resource wars, this other world force is talking about a sustainable future in which we rediscover an ancient respect for the natural world, and in which we create sustainable and just economic systems that acknowledge the singularity of this planet and recognize that its wealth was destined for the use of all.

In the face of the lack of vision of the developed world, the poor, the workers, campesinos, and indigenous people, making up the civil society of the Global South, are proposing a profound re-analysis of our world reality and are doing massive organizing around the resulting vision.

In Bolivia the Quechua and Aymara peoples have used this vision to unseat presidents who continued collaborating with the elites who have controlled the wealth of that country since pre-Hispanic times. They have forced companies (in this case Bechtel) who colluded with those presidents and privatized water at unaffordable prices to leave the country and have re-asserted the right of the people of Bolivia over their rich natural resources. They have elected Evo Morales as the first indigenous president in Bolivia's history, and he proclaims this an "epoch of triumph, of joy, and of fiesta . . . a democratic revolution with votes, not bullets. And we will do away with the colonial state." As we have seen, he proclaims, "The indigenous and original peoples of the world are the moral reserve of humanity."[17]

But instead of joining the party, those who favor trade and resource wars perceive such visions as a threat. The U.S. National Intelligence Council in its study entitled "Global Trends 2020 — Mapping the Global Future," depicts both indigenous activism in Latin America and Islamic radicalism as threats to the security and hegemony of the United States.[18]

In Colombia indigenous leaders such as Feliciano Valencia from the Association of Indigenous Councils of Northern Cauca respond, "We are not a threat to the world, or to the United States. On the contrary, we hold out a hope, an alternative for humanity."[19] Just a partial list of indigenous organizations, assembled by the International Relations Center reveals eighty indigenous groups in twenty countries of Latin America and the United States who hold out this hope and this alternative to us.[20]

In the Ecuadorian Amazon the Napo Runa people created a sophisticated cultivation method in their jungle environment, making use of their intimate knowledge of companion planting, and formed a balanced jungle ecosystem that served their needs and those of their companion jungle species. So delicately was it balanced with the natural environment that European explorers on first seeing it proclaimed it untouched, virgin jungle. Still in our day Ecuadorian governments have labeled the jungle uninhabited territory and opened it to non-indigenous settlers. The Napo Runa have defended their lands and hope to inspire the other cultures of the world by their example to develop similarly sophisticated interfaces with the planet, its environment, and its creatures on a global scale as an alternative to resource wars and trade battles.

In Mexico the indigenous Zapatistas, who marched into the plaza in San Cristóbal de las Casas in the state of Chiapas in 1994 and declared themselves in open rebellion against NAFTA and plans for the "death of the Indigenous peoples," have also stirred hope and offered alternatives that reassert indigenous values as the basis for a future economic and social "revolution" to meet the needs of the planet and its creatures in this twenty-first century.

And the Mixtecs, in a zero sum world, a world of limited "good," with their *tequios* and *guezas,* their *cargos* and their *mayordomias,* with their millennial agricultural knowledge and seeds, join in with this diverse community of visionaries who have become the second world super-power to outline a set of values that can build hopeful alternatives for all of us on this planet.

Chapter Ten

Exchanging Universes

Loving Unseen Possibilities for Change

Exchanging Universes

A few days ago a friend and I were leaving the newly reforested valleys of Tilantongo after a visit to Aaron Santiago and Fidelia. We had seen the still scarred and eroded slashes of red and white soil where the reforestation had not yet arrived but was planned for this coming year. And we had visited the new forests, now twenty years old, whose lush green shade foreshadowed the future of those "hopelessly" eroded slashes.

"Imagine," my friend exclaimed, "the feeling of being able to change so drastically the whole universe in which your life takes place!"

Indeed, I thought, the people of Tilantongo had decided some twenty years ago to change universes. Instead of living in a universe of ruined, rocky soils and diminishing springs in an ever deepening poverty reduced to repeating as a kind of self-fulfilling mantra, "We are a sad and unfortunate people," they decided to change universes. And, little by little, they have been doing just that.

If we in the United States want to participate in the new hope and the new world envisioned by the campesinos, the indigenous peoples, the workers, and the poor of the South that we learned of in the last chapter, we need to take on the challenge that the people of Tilantongo decided upon. We need to change universes. It may be difficult for us to imagine that we could change our "universe" in the United States to something ecologically sustainable, something that no longer relies on controlling the resources of other nations, something economically just that reflects the very best values that our nation has known. But in the beginning it was just as hard for the people of Tilantongo to imagine that they could turn dry ravines into forests and turn trickling springs into

The previous Mixtec universe

strong flows by recharging aquifers. They thought Aaron, Jesús, Fidelia, Fermina, and Fidel were out of their minds.

What would it look like if we, too, made the same decision as did the Mixtecs of Tilantongo? If we decided to change the universe in which we live? And where would we get the energy to make such a decision?

The Energy to Change

Our youngest son, Dominic, is the mechanic of the family. But he is also a kind of artist, and a sort of poet — an artist because he has the eye to see the beauty that is around him that most of us miss, and a poet because he knows how to communicate to people's souls with no masks to protect him. One day he was looking for a car part for a junked vehicle he had bought to get from Connecticut back home to New Mexico. He dickered with the man at the junkyard but still the man wanted more money than Dominic had. Finally, Dominic, a grin beginning to form on his face, looked at the man and said, "How about all the money I have and two apple pies?" A smile began to form on the junkman's face, too. He paused. Finally, through a broad smile, he said, "Okay!" And Dominic went home and baked two apple pies.

It was Dominic who told us the other day, "You know, Mom and Dad, you can't get these kinds of changes to happen by talking about being more responsible. People have more than enough obligations already. We have to change out of love." Indeed, Dominic! The creative energy, the passionate vision, the fierce perseverance necessary for the magnitude of change we need for this century can be generated only as we learn to love this planet, this creation, this green fountain of life, this people that we are as a human race. How do we learn to love the things that lead to a happy future, to peace with justice, to a sustainable respect for our mother planet? Surely this will require changes in us that are so deep that they must be called "spiritual" changes. No simple change of congresspeople or political parties, no slight policy adjustments will accomplish what needs to be done.

Perhaps first we will have to rid ourselves of the idea that to even suggest such a change of universe we would have to be out of touch with the "real world." The other day a friend was saying that he had to return to the real world, the world of the everyday work of running a business. Perhaps that is something like the "real world" in which many of us live. But I have heard friends who have been in prison adamantly insist that prison represented the "real world." Poor people in Chicago slums have told me that that was the "real world," as have poor campesino farmers about their everyday world. We need to remember that there are many versions of the "real world," all of them approximating something of the reality of life, but none exhausting the possibilities of life. Then we need to allow ourselves to experience an exhilarating sense of freedom as we set out on a new adventure to find the "real world" that is worth our loving it.

At a college presentation a few years ago Mexican bishop Samuel Ruiz, who had worked in indigenous communities in the state of Chiapas, upon completing his discourse was approached by a young North American student who, overcome by the challenges posed by Ruiz's description of the state of the world, simply asked, "What should I do?" Ruiz gazed at the young man and said, "Only two things. First, you need to be willing to think differently than everyone else in this auditorium. Because there is a current of thinking here that will not let you see what you need to see. And second, you need to go live with the poor to learn to see things from their perspective." That was all!

Indeed, as a nation, our vision has been clouded by fear, by chauvinism, and by pride. What a gift it would be to be able to see beyond to the rich kaleidoscope of peoples and cultures with all of their color and value that make up our human family, peoples and cultures neither to be feared nor to be dominated. How freeing it would be to see beyond the scarce resources that make up the basic wealth of our planet and see the original beauty and bounty with which all of the life on this earth was gifted. How might we exercise our combined responsibility as the only known consciousness of this unique place in the universe and fall in love once again with who we are, all of us the peoples of the planet, and with the other creatures with whom we share this green and blue globe of a home that spins, silent and unique, in this corner of space.

It was the Christian mystic Saint Augustine who counseled, "Love God and do as you please." Could we learn to love this planet, its peoples, its living things, its fearful beauty? Could that be the first step in following Samuel Ruiz's advice to think differently? As Dominic says, it is doubtful that the energy we need for the magnitude of change that is needed will come from a sense of obligation. Allowing ourselves to love this earth as our ancient ancestors probably did could be the first step in learning a way to a sustainable world and a happier future for us all.[1]

If we can thus begin to see this world with new eyes, we may have fulfilled Samuel Ruiz's first recommendation to the young man who asked, "What should I do?" And although it is no substitute for living among the poor, we have tried to respect his second recommendation in the pages above and to pass on a glimpse into the world and the worldview of a portion of the world's marginalized people in the villages of the Mixteca Alta. Is there something more we can do?

The Voice of Indigenous America

"The white people do not understand our way of life. They don't know how to distinguish between one piece of land and another, for they are strangers who come in the night and take what land they need. The earth is not their sister but their enemy. They treat their mother, the earth, and their brother, the firmament, as objects to be bought. Their appetite will devour the land leaving behind only a desert. They contaminate their own bed, and one night they will perish choked in their own waste."[2]

That is the way the North American indigenous visionary Chief Seattle described the enterprise we call the American way over a century and a half ago. Perhaps today, with the help of indigenous Mixtec friends we are ready to hear what he had to say. Western European civilization, as expressed in the United States today, has come to a crossroads. It has become clear that some of its fundamental assumptions and directions over the past five hundred years are unsustainable, if not suicidal.

We need to let this fact help us to become reflective enough to think differently. Reflective enough to understand what we really want from life, and analytical enough to choose the lifestyle, the technologies, the values, and the politics that will get us there.

The problem is that we may not know what we want of life until we see it. That is the point of using another culture, in this case the Mixtec people, to stimulate our imaginations as to what unseen or unimagined possibilities our lives might contain. What unseen or unimagined possibilities emerge from our story?

1. The life and the work of the people of El Progreso Tilantongo show us that it is possible to resist the efforts of the economic elite of the West to redefine us, human persons, as *homo consumiens*. We are not what we consume, and consuming is not our reason for being. The people who took it upon themselves to change their "universe" with water-catching ditches and millions of native trees show us that creative work, participation in the process of creation, molding the earth into a more beautiful and enduring reality fulfill the yearning of our souls and the needs of the planet far more than shopping at the mall. Diarmuid O'Murchu points out that this creativity is deep in our history and nature:

> Already, two million years ago, we were behaving as creative, innovative creatures. A sense of being engaged with the surrounding creation is clearly in place, hence the appellation *Homo ergaster* (the human worker), commonly used in the relevant literature. Creativity is built into our very makeup. It is a vital clue not just to our survival, but also in the search for meaning that we have pursued for at least two million years.[3]

The people of Tilantongo combine with the ancient sages of the age of Quetzalcóatl to suggest to us that it is not in having more things that we find happiness. Even if every fifty-two years our consumer luxuries were snatched from us as happened with the ancient indigenous temples and their artwork, we could indeed feel fulfilled and affirmed if we were able to be part of a creative process that helped shape the planet into something more just, more peaceful, and more enduring.

We need to imagine a world in which we are not primarily consumers and in which we do not equate happiness with having. And in the twenty-first century imagining and creating such a world may be necessary for our survival as a species.

The new Mixtec universe where the old once stood

2. Endless growth, in modern economic terms, is not an option. It is perhaps because the ancient Mixtec people did not demand such growth as a part of their social and economic foundations that they have survived as a culture for five thousand years. Citing the successful one-thousand-year-old history of the Pueblo Indians of our own Southwest, and the six-hundred-year-long endurance of the Chaco Canyon civilizations in New Mexico, which collapsed due to environmental pressures, Jared Diamond, in *Collapse*, concludes, "That should make us modern Americans hesitate to be too confident yet about the sustainability of our First World economy, especially when we reflect how quickly Chaco society collapsed after its peak in the decade A.D. 1110–20, and how implausible the risk of collapse would have seemed to the Chacoans of that decade."[4]

The world's indigenous societies need to lead us to see the possibilities of an economic world that does not demand constant growth. In fact, to survive this century we must find ways to simplify our needs and find alternatives to economies that subscribe to the doctrine of unending growth.

3. *Tequio, guezta, cargos, mayordomias,* and communal landholding have no doubt been part of what has helped the Mixtec culture survive

multiple invasions, climate changes, and ecological disasters for over five thousand years. All of these mechanisms for assuring the common good and avoiding undue accumulation of wealth have their survival value for sustainable societies. Village authorities assign parcels of communal land to families and individuals. These individual plots of land give room for the essential inventiveness and inspiration of the individual in his or her own sphere within the framework of communal land ownership. U.S. culture maintains that economic progress is built upon the strength of the independent, self-made individual. But our "greatest" self-made individuals and corporations ignore their total dependence on the social fabric in which they work and onto which they often externalize the costs of their success. The ideology of the "isolated individual" and the "isolated nation" pursuing their own personal riches as if they were not part of an interdependent whole on this limited planet may represent the greatest danger to our survival as a species in this the twenty-first century.

We must learn a model of solidarity that works for us as a community of individuals and as a community of nations. Our actions must affirm the actual solidarity and interdependence that exists between all species on a planet that now challenges us to amend together the "contaminating of our own bed." We need to build new ways of working for the common good, a common good on which we all depend for our individual and national survival in a world that increasingly demands moderate and shared use of its vast but limited ability to create and sustain life.

4. We will need all the wisdom and insight that the still colorful array of cultures and world visions can provide us in order for the human community to succeed at this new task of solidarity for our mutual good and that of the other species with whom we share the planet. The insight of the Mixtec peoples represents a tiny fraction of the wealth of wisdom that the diverse cultures of the human world still have to offer us as we attempt to create a different vision of society more appropriate to our fragile ecological and social situation on the planet.

We need to value and promote, ask advice from, and marvel at the wisdom that the diverse cultures of the world continue to offer us and free ourselves from reliance on the illusion that American monoculture provides either an example for all or a viable solution to the primary problems our world faces in this century. Once having dispelled the illusion of our own superior readiness for the task at hand, we will more easily defend ourselves against U.S. politicians who insist that it is in our best interest to dominate the peoples and cultures of the world for our own ends.

5. Some Mixtec farmers, when they arrive at their fields guiding the ox team with its hand-crafted oak plow, still pause a moment. They address themselves to the Mother Earth, and they ask permission for the intrusion into the living cap of the Mother's soil that the plow will cut with its furrows. A growing number of modern physicists, cosmologists, ecologists, and religious thinkers agree with this perception that the earth is much more like a living organism than a dead rock. Indeed, the evolution story clearly places us as a product of the whole of the natural community, a part of a living family that extends far beyond the limits of the human.

Crossing the rolling hills of the northern Mixteca Alta one day, I came to a sudden precipice that dropped into a vast space of pine-covered canyon. Far below in a valley crafted to overwhelm the human spirit with its immensity and to tantalize the mind with pregnant meaning, lay the city of Apoala. This valley, lush with underground lakes, flowing streams and waterfalls in the midst of a semi-arid land cradles the history of creation for the Mixtecs. According to Mixtec cosmology, two *ahuehuetes,* or water cypress trees, swaying over the waters of Apoala fell in love. They loved each other so that they wanted to create something beautiful together, and so they created the first human being, the first Mixtec. There is a mural of this first human child floating on a lotus flower in the waters of Apoala in the Palacio Presidencial in the capital city of Oaxaca.

The Mixtec story perhaps more accurately represents our birth from the community of nature and our membership in the larger natural community than our own creation stories. If we are to make our peace with this larger community and understand that *it will not* be treated simply as a tool for human adventure, pleasure, or profit, we must learn to find our fulfillment as members of this larger, intensely rich and diverse community of life. We must extend the respect that the Mixtec children talk about as an essential part of their culture to the full community of life. We must let that respect permeate our spiritual, economic, and political life if we hope to be around at the close of the century.

All of this will represent such an intimate change of perspective for our society and for each of us individuals that we would have to call it spiritual. A complete change of worldview is necessary if we are to successfully "change universes" as the people of Tilantongo have done. How can we learn to love the values inherent in this new way of being?

Chapter Eleven

A Special Time of Hope

The "Mixtec Principles"
and What They Suggest for Us

From what we have seen in the villages of the Mixteca Alta with Jesús and Fermina, Agustín, and Fidel and Fidelia, we can distill some distinct principles for a different kind of future. You may have been able to distill other things from our visits also. But some such principles could be:

1. The *Cargo* principle insists that leadership exists primarily to serve the community.

2. The principle of the *Limited Good* insists that on a limited planet, the distribution, not the accumulation, of wealth will be the primary economic challenge of our future.

3. The *Tequio* principle suggests that community work for the common good will be the second key economic concept that will assure our common future.

4. The *Earth Mother* principle recognizes that we are part of the earth's family, not its controllers, and we must learn to treat the rest of our family members, human and non-human, with respect.

5. The *Ancestor* principle reminds us that we are part of an ongoing creative process building upon the shoulders of our human and evolutionary ancestors who ask us to take our part in the historic development of the planet.

With these principles in mind, we can sketch the outlines of suggestions that can help us envision a different kind of future for our nation and our planet.[1]

Planting native trees, planting hope

A New Kind of Politics

We may be beginning to emerge from a period in our human history thousands of years old in which the strong and the wealthy have been our leaders.[2] They represent a part of humanity that is addicted to power and control, and they have led us into endless power struggles, culminating in the European- and American-led slaughter of hundreds of millions of our species in the twentieth and early twenty-first centuries. Violence, indeed, forms an essential strategy of their leadership practice. But it is not an essential part of the way of being of the ordinary villagers, farmers, and city-dwellers of the human species.

Service, not control, must be the raison d'être of politics in our future. For this to happen people with a will to serve must offer themselves as candidates for office, while at the same time we must eliminate the political incentives that attract those addicted to power. Politics must cease to be an opportunity for personal enrichment. This may mean reduced government salaries and the elimination of opportunities to collude for personal gain. And campaign reform must eliminate the role of large moneyed interests in the election process.

A New Kind of Civil Society

The kind of activism we see today among indigenous peoples and campesino organizations across Latin America is not foreign to U.S. culture. The nineteenth and early twentieth centuries in the United States were characterized by energetic and inventive worker movements that, though often brutally suppressed, achieved many of the benefits that U.S. workers still enjoyed until the reactionary reforms of the 1970s and 1980s.

When the Industrial Workers of the World, also known as the Wobblies, were prohibited from speaking on the streets of Missoula, Montana, in 1918 by a clearly unconstitutional town ordinance, the IWW called on workers from across the West. So many street speakers appeared to take the "podium" that the town's jails soon overflowed. Organizers timed speakers so as to assure arrests just before dinner time and throw the burden of feeding the multitudes on the city budget. Within a few short weeks Missoula's city council rescinded the unconstitutional ordinance. We need such imagination and humor in our own organizing of civil society. We had a great burst of such creative energy in the 1960s and new signs of imagination in the demonstrations of the present century.

Mexican campesino leader Pedro Torres perhaps explains best the type of organizing mentality we need for the twenty-first century in which gargantuan economic powers are pressuring our political systems from above. He recounts that when his organization, the Democratic Campesino Front of Chihuahua (Frente Democrático Campesino de Chihuahua), occupies municipal or state assemblies with their demonstrations, they tell the authorities, "We are not against you. We are here to help you do what you really want to do for your community. We understand that you receive strong pressures from above to do things that are not in the interests of your community and that you need stronger pressure from below to enable you to do the right thing. We are here to give you that pressure and help you to do what is right."

We presently have at our disposal a multitude of new technologies that can help us to help elected leaders to do the "right thing." In recent history, Spanish citizens successfully organized against a government that was lying to them about the causes of a terrorist attack on Madrid trains. They convened over a million people in twenty-four hours, using the Internet and cell phones. In elections two days later they were able to turn out of office the government responsible for the untruths. Venezuelan popular movements foiled a coup attempt against their president, using fax machines and cell phones.

We have at our fingertips the tools and the information for a new kind of citizen participation in the democratic process. We need to find the will to use them as the indigenous and campesino movements have done.

A New Kind of Science and Technology

The campesinos of Tilantongo have seen an array of technological "solutions" to their agricultural challenges come and go. For this reason, they have grown far less likely than we to buy each new solution that Western science and technology might propose. They are able to analyze what they want out of life, what resources they have at their disposal to achieve it, and to choose or devise technology appropriate to their aspirations and resource base.

If we look a little more closely at the case of the wild edible *quelites* in Mexican fields that we mentioned earlier, we see that at present our Western sciences tend to omit this very basic kind of analysis. Last year at a meeting of campesino men and women, the women spoke up about agricultural technology. "Our men," they pronounced, "like herbicides. But that's because they are lazy. We women know that there is a whole array of wild edible plants and greens that grow only in our cultivated fields and that provide a huge source of free, nutritious food for our families. We call them *quelites*. Herbicides wipe out this important source of free food."

As we have seen, this phenomenon is not restricted to the Mexican *campo*. Parts of Asia now suffer from high incidences of incurable blindness due to vitamin A deficiencies. If we were to seriously look for the causes of these recent deficiencies, we would need to ask what has changed in the nutritional makeup of the Asian diet. Two things would stand out. The processing that produces white rice removes the germ of the rice and results in a diet low in natural vitamins and minerals. The second factor we would notice is the elimination by the application of herbicides of green, leafy, wild greens (*quelites*), one of the best sources of vitamin A and other vitamins to be found in the human diet.

Our modern agricultural science, however, has developed a solution to this problem (the "miracle" genetically modified golden rice, high in vitamin A) that completely ignores its causes. This kind of science chooses to overlook its own role in causing the problem by introducing processed rice and herbicides. The new solution, of course, leads to dependence on outside sources of seed and the need for farmers to buy seed each growing season.

Not only does our present style of agricultural science ignore the social and environmental effects of its inventions; it often sets us up for
catastrophe by refusal to examine what resources we really have at our
disposal in the long run.

The "green revolution" style of agriculture that the farmers of Tilantongo are in the process of rejecting, after decades of often disappointing
experience, was built upon the understanding that to progress biologically to plants that could produce more food per plant, we had to develop
plants that could absorb and use more nitrogen, one of the key sub-
stances responsible for plant growth. But to increase the ability of such
plants to absorb and use such quantities of nitrogen without toxic results, we needed to develop plants that could, and in fact would need to,
absorb much greater quantities of water than our normal food plants.
Green revolution agricultural science thus developed new varieties of
plants that could absorb these unusual quantities of water.[3]

Yet today we are being forced to recognize the limited availability
of fresh water. Currently 1.2 billion people live without access to clean
water. Of all the fresh water used on the planet, already 70 percent of
it is used in agriculture, not campesino agriculture primarily, but "green
revolution"–style agriculture. As we stretch the limits of our fresh water
supplies, agricultural technologies that rely on excessive quantities of
water are not the answer for feeding the world in the future.

A corporate science and technology so narrowly focused on technical innovation or directed by the tyranny of quarterly profits does not
see its human, dietary, social, and long-term environmental and resource
impacts. In the search for short-term profits, such impacts are externalized onto the generations of our children and grandchildren. This sort
of science and technology will not get us through the present century.

We need a science and a technology able to do the kind of analysis
that Tilantongo's farmers do, a science and technology that interacts with
our communities and our environment, is conscious of its historical and
social consequences, and frees itself from its ties to corporate profits
in order to assist us with foresighted and long-term solutions to real
problems. Such a science and technology must be able to recognize and
critique its own negative social, economic, and environmental impacts.

A New Kind of Economy

The Mixtec culture realized early on that in a world of limited good,
the distribution of wealth was a key to cultural survival. So they built

in mechanisms to control the flow of wealth and to assure a common good. In our Western world of today accumulation has become a rogue, marauding through our world social body and threatening the good of the species and the planet.

Unregulated or underregulated transnational corporations have developed into the leading edge of this threat to the global common good. Much of the impetus for the founding of the United States came from the desire of the colonists to free themselves from the overwhelming power of British corporations. The Boston Tea Party encapsulates the spirit of the Declaration of Independence. It was primarily an anti-corporate demonstration aimed at British firms, and early U.S. law was designed to control the development of such dangerous corporate power in the new republic.

Though some corporations do good things, a world in which corporations, whose primary responsibility is to the profits of their stockholders, determine our politics, our economic choices, our science, our self-concept, and our vision for the future is not viable.

Corporations require firm government regulation at a time when deregulation has become part of government economic and trade policy, and many transnational corporations rival or surpass entire nations in economic power, seriously compromising the global common good.

Today corporate power strangles our public institutions and the world's economies. Serious anti-trust legislation and labor legislation was systematically dismantled in the United States during the 1970s and 1980s to prepare for the corporate free trade and market liberalization of the 1990s. Overproducing for the U.S. market and running out of cheap labor on the domestic scene, U.S. corporations needed unrestricted access to foreign markets and to foreign cheap labor. Increased access to foreign labor and markets was used to further undermine U.S. labor's power and to consolidate corporate control of our political life and public policy.

On the international level, corporate power combined with governmental support is devastating. Not so long ago, while the G8 (Group of eight countries controlling around two-thirds of the world's economy) was debating what sort of economic aid could help Africa to pull itself out of its deepening poverty, Naomi Klein wrote an article pointing out that Africa really didn't so much need the small aid the wealthy countries were willing to give, as it needed to be freed from the stranglehold of foreign corporations. Africa is rich in natural resources from oil to diamonds, gold to copper. The problem is that foreign corporations exploiting this wealth leave less than 10 percent of the profits behind for the African nations whose resources they are. A friend working in Tanzania reported that the Tanzanians' share of the profits on their gold, mined by South African corporations, is only 3 percent. "After the last round of [World Trade Organization] trade negotiations, rich countries estimated that they would gain by $141.8 billion per year and Africa would be $2.6 billion per year worse off."[4] At home and abroad we must find ways to break the stranglehold that these immensely powerful corporations wield over our common life.

Corporate appetite threatens our planet's future. We need to apply the lessons of the Mixteca. We must distribute our resource use among our human community in socially sustainable ways, while we also distribute our resource use over time in order to respect the needs of the planet and its future generations.

On a personal level, we must learn economic habits that are socially and environmentally sustainable. That responsibility rests primarily with the American and Western European people who are practicing and promoting in the rest of the world a way of life that undermines the life-giving potential of the planet. We are the unsustainable element of the human family and not the example to follow.

A New Kind of Education

I was in the guidance office of a large Midwestern university using the phone last year when I picked up a sheet of paper and began to read the list of the career opportunities that awaited the discriminating graduate of the institution. It listed about twenty choices of professional and corporate options of what you could do with your life, once you had your degree in hand. "What a depressing way to look at the possibilities that a life holds!" I thought to myself.

The possibilities of a creative life are, of course, so much richer than any list of professions. But our educational systems limit themselves to promoting and accrediting distinction to only a small minority of those options. This is partly why we produce scientists and professionals who lack the ability that the campesino of Tilantongo has to analyze options, determine what he or she wants out of life, and match technology and resource use to those goals. It is also part of the reason why we have lost our creativity and, often, our excitement about life.

A new kind of education will recognize the unlimited diversity and richness of the universe in which we live. It will celebrate the mystery of human consciousness and the unfathomable evolutionary processes that have given birth to this consciousness. And it will have all the reason in the universe to believe in the direction of the process that has produced the incredible complexity, richness, and beauty of a human person or a galaxy. It will recognize the limits of any specialized study, and it will long to link its knowledge and skill with the wider human experience of all of the cultures of the world, to help us all determine what it is we want out of this human life, together and as individuals, and what we really need to achieve what we have decided upon.

A New Kind of Work

Following the tree-planters of Tilantongo, who chose to work to exchange a universe of dry, eroded hillsides for one of deep forests and rich and growing soils, we must place much more hope in our work. Our evolutionary story tells us that we are part of the same creation process that has produced our planet and cosmos. Our lives have immense creative possibilities within this ongoing history.

To work just for the money should come to be considered an antisocial behavior in our time. And our sense of personal fulfillment must have the vision to link itself to the larger directions of the historical process, both human and planetary. We are co-creators and our educational systems as well as the ways we are raised must first of all prepare us for that kind of creative thought and work. Our intellectual, our scientific, and our physical work need to be guided by this call we have to join with the rich reality of human life options and cultures and the momentum of the universe to create an even richer future.

A New Kind of Ecology

Much of our thinking and our policies about ecology and the environment arise from our European/American mind-set. Our environmentalists have rightly perceived that the European-based economic, scientific, and intellectual societies of today cannot coexist with nature. A society that, at the level of its most fundamental intellectual presuppositions, believes it has a mission to subdue the other life forms that surround it and extract the resources of the globe to overcome whatever stands in the way of human growth and resource consumption will find itself at war with its own home, with the very life force on which it depends for its existence.

One of the chief techniques our U.S. environmental organizations have promoted to solve this dilemma is to establish "reserves." Reserves attempt to set aside places where human beings will not be able to enter and engage in this destructive behavior that threatens the very home on which we depend.

Curiously, there is now evidence that the nature reserve concept does not solve the problem. Studies in some regions of Latin America, where areas of high biodiversity have been set aside in reserves, show extinction rates of species as high or higher within reserves as outside of reserves, partly because of their isolation from the larger environmental systems that provide the biological interchange necessary to the survival of diverse species. Some scientists are now suggesting that instead of reserves we need to develop environmental grids or matrices under the supervision of campesinos and indigenous peoples that can provide corridors of natural flow for native species to promote the kind of interchange that can preserve and promote diversity. In such matrices we will have to learn how to live at peace with our fellow species.[5]

The Noa Romi people of the jungles of Ecuador, mentioned previously, may be a good model of the type of human behavior that can indeed live with the natural world on which we depend for our sustenance.

We desperately need to rethink the fundamental lines of our intellectual history and investigate and understand the intellectual foundations of indigenous cultures such as the Mixtecs and the Noa Romi if we are to make it through this next century. For societies that have for so long considered themselves intellectually superior to the non-white societies of the world, this may take serious self-examination. But Jesús and Fidel and Fermina and our other Mixtec friends who have introduced us to the rich world of the indigenous cultures assure us it will be an exciting and invigorating journey.

A New Kind of Religion

We are at a time in the history of human society in which, at the same time as there is polarization among religious traditions and we have arrived, once again, at the extreme of killing one another in the name of God, there is also a current of experience that is recognizing our closeness across religious barriers. At a deep spiritual level we are recognizing a common consciousness between the respect for the Divine in nature of the indigenous peoples, the love of peace and the deep sense for the human spirit of the Hindu and Buddhist sages, the poetic vision of the loveable universe of the Sufi holy ones, and the universal love taught by the Jesus of Christian spirituality. What we are learning about the vast and magnificent process of cosmic creation that has brought forth life on this small planet may be leading us to a new maturity. This maturity will allow us to admit that the Divine that we seek is so much vaster than we had ever imagined and so much beyond our individual and cultural ability to capture, that we are all, in our various spiritual traditions, no doubt seeing and expressing only a tiny part of that total reality we call the Divine. We have been in the habit of mistaking a fleeting glimpse of the Divine for the whole and of declaring our vision the only valid one.

A new religious perspective for our time will embrace the human family's great diversity of glimpses of the Divine across cultures and over time. It will see the great variety of experience of the holy that the human family has received as stimulating and freeing, much as the glimpse into the cultural richness of the Mixtec people has been for some of us. Our spiritual directions need to be free of claims to exclusivity, free of proselytizing, and they need to expand beyond centering on ritual. We need to take on a new calling to aid our human family in its search for the deepest meaning of our combined evolution and creation story. Our formal religions need to take the lead, especially in an era of destructive nationalism, to declare our fundamental nature as family — family with the infinite variety of human beings and human cultures, with the vast variety of living beings with whom we share this home, and with the living planet, the Earth Mother herself.

And a Very Old Way...

All this can happen only as we heal our relations with ourselves and our home in the universe. Diarmuid O'Murchu suggests that we were not always an alienated species.[6] Perhaps our ancient ancestors resembled some of our indigenous family members of today, who feel at home with the planet, feel at home with our other family members in nature, and even feel at home with death, as do the Mixtec communities. May these meditations through which the Mixtec communities have led us help us to recapture a very old way of being at home in and in love with our world and our cosmos.

Chapter Twelve

Happiness and
a Sustainable World

How Can We Respond to the Invitation
of Indigenous Peoples and the Global South?

Steve recounted a recent visit to the mountains of Oaxaca.

A month ago I visited the extremely remote region of Santiago Ixtayutla, a zone bordering between the Mixtec and Chatino peoples.
At 5:00 one morning a small group of four of us left to visit a
tiny mountainside community called Corral de Piedra. I drove our
small white two-wheel-drive pickup as far as it would go, and we
walked the last ninety minutes along a steep mountain trail guided
by Isaac, a campesino whom we met walking on the road. During our walk, we ran into an older campesino dressed in the loose
white cotton shirt and pants worn by the indigenous of the region. This was Don Aurelio. I noticed that while older than me by
some twenty years, Don Aurelio walked with stamina and grace.
I sweated and stumbled even as I watched the ease with which he
climbed. I carried a plastic bottle of water, which he offered to
carry for me in his pouch. Since I had already dropped the bottle twice, I agreed. It turned out that this man was known as a
tatamandon of the area, a wise elder. He joined us at our brief
gathering at the community-based store we visited. He also spoke
first in response to any questions; that is the role of the ranking
tatamandon. When, the meeting ended I looked to Don Aurelio for
my water bottle. "Oh," he said, "I left it below."

I followed him down "below," a few hundred feet down the
mountainside. We arrived at a leveled area occupied by a clean,

A future for all

small simple chapel. And there, leaning by the side of the door in the shade, I saw and collected my water bottle. But first we reverently entered the chapel. It began to dawn on me that our *tatamandon* host used my water bottle to arrange our coming here after the meeting. Any important visit must include a moment to visit the town's sacred space. As we left the chapel, he took his leave, telling us to return to our truck by a lower and easier path than the one we used in our arrival. I said, "Thank you." He responded, "Primero Dios," shook my hand, smiled and briskly headed back up the mountain. Primero Dios — "God before all else." The phrase means various things to Oaxacans. It can be a reminder to get our priorities straight. Some things, in this case our relation to the Divine, are more important than others. It can also simply be a recognition that even for a next meeting or an additional day in our lives we depend on forces far beyond our control. In the context of Oaxacan indigenous society Don Aurelio was stating a truth about life that is almost universally recognized by indigenous people here but that we have trouble with in our society: the truth that, to a large degree, if we are realistic about our place in the universe, we are not in control of our lives.

Of course, there are differences on the continuum of control that we might have, and, to a significant degree, the poor and the rich occupy different positions on that scale. Don Aurelio's acknowledgement that we are never sure, nor in control of whether we will see one another again, could be a more realistic assessment than what we often assume about how much control we actually have in this world. And this, in turn, also says something about how much lack of control he and we are content to live with.

Steve continued,

Twenty years ago, I returned to work in the United States after a period in Caracas, Venezuela, where I worked in a barrio slum called Nuevo Horizonte. The team I worked with there paid close attention not only to what we did, but also how we did it. In each of our activities, we tried our best to work with local people who were helping build people's capacity to organize and lead them-selves. We referred to this as "empowering" the people. We had concluded that our neighbors suffered in large part because they lacked sufficient power to decide about their lives, to care for their families, to work, to recreate. Too little control undermined their human capacities.

Many expatriates who work in another culture find the adjustment back to United States culture difficult, and it was for me, too. What surprised me was where I found the kindred spirits I needed to help me reintegrate. I found them in twelve-step-based self-help groups. There I found middle-class and upper-middle-class people working very hard to recuperate and heal from a diversity of physical, emotional, and spiritual illnesses. They were striving to recover wholeness in their lives. These people and groups embraced a disciplined practice of the twelve steps which form the foundation of Alcoholics Anonymous. They found that following these steps, originally designed to help people recover from alcohol addiction, also helped them recover from other physical, emotional, and spiritual maladies.[1] The key to this approach was coming to accept that you were not in control of significant parts of your life.

The poor often have less control than they need over the basic necessities of their lives, while we who are well off often have an unrealistically inflated sense of our own control that can become pathological when we encounter experiences that clearly demonstrate our lack of control.

Seventy-two percent of the workforce here in the state of Oaxaca earns less than $7.00 per day. A quart of milk costs $1.50; a round-trip city bus fare costs another 70 cents. This is not enough money to adequately feed a family, let alone access adequate health care or provide for an education for children. Most parents in Oaxaca cannot provide enough for their children to grow and thrive. Nearly 3 billion of the earth's inhabitants earn far less than Oaxacans, less than two dollars a day. Clearly the poor lack enough control over their lives even to provide the beginnings of a dignified lifestyle for their children.

On the other hand, do we in the United States have an unrealistic sense of our own control and can this become pathological? We have trouble as a people coming to terms with two basic realities: we are all going to die, and in spite of our most responsible projections, most disciplined life choices, despite our best researched purchases, things are going to happen to us and to our families that we do not want to have happen. The unreasonable assumption behind our U.S. penchant for suing one another is that all things can and therefore should be under control. The sidewalks should have no irregularities that could cause a fall. A dog should not get out of control and bite someone and the hot water served in a restaurant should not be hot enough to burn us if we should spill it. Our attempts to sue away danger and mishaps or to avoid them by unreasonable amounts of insurance belie an unrealistic wish, and to an extent an expectation, that people can be kept from all danger and harm.

Our demand for insurance against the vagaries of life, particularly liability insurance, certainly provides a boon for lawyers and the insurance industry, but it also makes simple activities of nonprofits, who for instance sponsor reality trips to other cultures and countries, difficult because of liability risk. Someone one day might trip on a sidewalk, perhaps in Kenya or Mexico City and sue the sponsoring organization, claiming that we should have avoided that sidewalk. Far too often, these cases win but even if they don't, the innocent and defending party must pay significant legal fees. It is sometimes only from outside our culture of control in countries that do not have such unrealistic expectations of control and risk avoidance that we can see that our need for control does not coincide with the conditions of life.

As North Americans we tend to seek to remedy our discomfort with the lack of control which, in spite of the unrealistic hope we place in lawsuits and insurance, we keep encountering in our lives through a drive to buy, possess, and protect things and to isolate ourselves from threats to our control in suburbs and gated communities.

The notion of shopping as a defense against threats to our control was taken to extremes by President George W. Bush after the attacks of September 11, 2001, on New York and Washington, DC. Benjamin Wallace-Wells in his October 2003 article in the *Washington Monthly* writes: "On September 20, in his first lengthy national address after the [September 11] attacks, Bush told the citizens of the United States what they personally could do: 'Live your lives and hug your children,' he said. Be patient with FBI investigations and travel delays, and 'your continued participation and confidence in the American economy' would be greatly appreciated. Telling Americans to go shopping, however, didn't exactly stir the nation's patriotic blood."[2] The president urged us to go shopping as a way to heal from the greatest national tragedy in the living memory of most U.S citizens. September 11 illustrated to us that we are not invulnerable and to remedy this sense of vulnerability, our nation's top leader encouraged us to go shopping, as though the nation would find solace and peace and security in the act of shopping, purchasing, consuming.

At the same time we have a strong tendency to try to remedy the lack of control of our collective future with an aggressive and violent nationalism. George Kennan, then State Department Staff Chief, said it very bluntly in February of 1948:

> We have about 50 per cent of the world's wealth but only 6.3 per cent of its population. In this situation we cannot fail to be the object of envy and resentment. Our real task in the coming period is to devise a pattern of relationships which will permit us to maintain this position of disparity. We need not deceive ourselves that we can afford today the luxury of altruism and world benefaction. We should cease to talk about such vague and unreal objectives as human rights, the raising of living standards and democratization. The day is not far off when we are going to have to deal in straight power concepts. The less we are then hampered by idealistic slogans, the better.[3]

But perhaps more than we would like to believe, that same reaction to a potential lack of control of our future has become a part of our national psyche. We are at war in Iraq. We remedy the lack of control of our collective future (in this case access to petroleum) with an aggressive and violent nationalism which we call "national security." We initiate wars and kill citizens of other countries in a desperate effort to prolong our way of life, a way of life, objectively speaking that is not sustainable. Even if such behavior doesn't appear pathological to us it does appear so to a great deal of the rest of the world.

Both poverty, if it entails the lack of the basic necessities of life, and overabundance of material goods affect the human spirit. Our temptation is to believe that accumulation of goods and resources will free us from the basic insecurities of life over which we have little control. In recent years we have been manipulated by our national leadership into a search for a security and control, such as that for which Mr. Kennan wished. The degree of control we would like to have is, realistically, unobtainable. In addition, even the control that a peaceful and sustainable world might provide us *is unobtainable as long as we continue to expect to capture such a disproportionate share of the world's resources for ourselves.* And yet we are paying dearly in lost freedoms and lost happiness for this quixotic quest for control.

Some people in both poor and wealthy countries have found innovative ways be free of these pathologies, to live more simply, in ways that enhance the quality of their lives while doing their part to reduce the damage that unchecked accumulation and resource use wreak on our planet.

When I gave the eulogy at **Greg Jaurequi's** funeral I said, "You know, Greg could be hard to get along with sometimes. But he was that way because he was determined not to let anyone step on 'his people,' the Chicano people of the U.S. Southwest." Greg grew up in New Mexico when the divide between Mexicans and Anglos created by white racism was as deep as that between blacks and whites in the Deep South. But Greg escaped the destiny of most of his people in Silver City and went to college in Denver, Colorado. He graduated with a degree in business and a promising career ahead. But instead he talked his young wife into "one last visit" to the Silver City of his youth. And he, unlike many others with such advantages, was captivated by the struggles of the Mexican people in the unions and in the streets of southern New Mexico, and he stayed. The family bought a large abandoned adobe house and worked to fix it up while they offered hospitality to the homeless of the area. Greg got a job with the government poverty program and settled in for a life-long struggle to help "his people" reassert their culture and emerge from a poverty rate that is still the highest in the country. Greg died early, but, as one friend said, "Greg was having the time of his life working for 'his people.'"

Ron and Shirley Black live in Atlanta, Georgia. Both graduated from college and Ron studied political science and expected to teach. Instead, when he married Shirley, he assumed leadership in Shirley's family business. Ron surprised himself with his own business skills, and under his direction, the family business grew rapidly. Another corporation approached Ron with an offer to buy the family company and income from the sale well compensated all of the family members involved in founding and running the business.

But instead of being content with their success, Shirley and Ron set aside a significant portion of their own gain and created a family foundation. They live in the same house, though they could have moved to a much more expensive home. Each year they meet with their four grade-school- and high-school-aged children to discuss and decide which causes and projects they will support that year with the funding that the foundation provides. Ron continues to work, but in a faith-based not-for-profit where his considerable talents are dedicated to service.

Jesús León is a campesino from the Mixteca Alta who was, ironically, born in one of the biggest urban centers in the world, Mexico City. When he was a few years old his folks moved back to their tiny home village of San Isidro Tilantongo and reestablished the farm. Jesús grew up and loved the land. And he also loved books. He went back to school as an adult and finished high school in nearby Nochixtlán. Although with his "smarts" and education he could have gotten a decent job in the city, he chose to stay with his campesino companions and form an organization to rebuild the Mixtec countryside. "We are not campesinos because we are too ignorant to do anything else!" I have often heard him say to encourage people in the struggle. "We are campesinos because it is our vocation, and because we have a historic knowledge of our soils and our seeds that we have from our ancestors. All the Mexican people depend on us for their food." The other day he told me, "You know, when I go to my brothers' houses in Mexico City, we can't talk to each other anymore. They have all the trinkets and gadgets that the money from their jobs can buy. But I can't understand what they see in those things. And when I talk to them about the campesino struggle for control over markets or about how we are preserving our seeds and our culture, they have no interest." But Jesús works unceasingly for a vision of a new Mixteca Alta, one in which the Mixtec culture builds upon its strengths and creates, once again, a land from which the young will no longer migrate. And Jesús is happy.

Samantha Bennett describes herself as a "soccer mom," but she contributes much more to her community in Oroville, California, than that. One of her children is disabled. Some time ago, she decided with her husband, Jeff, that they would live off the salary he made and that, instead of pursuing paid work, Samantha would dedicate herself to care of the family and active contribution to community life. Samantha's service has included work on school boards, in local politics, at church, in cultural fund raisers, and efforts to build awareness and support for the disabled.

Not too long ago Samantha also took advantage of an opportunity to visit with poor families along the U.S.–Mexico border and her life was touched by the people she met there simply struggling to meet daily needs. Samantha is a very concrete and practical person, and when she returned home, the first thing she did was clean out her closets and simplify her own life. Later, to her children's dismay, she and her husband also worked to "simplify" Christmas and to redirect focus from the quantity of gifts and instead make Christmas a celebration of gratitude for life.

Samantha also says that she will be having new and different conversations with all of the other soccer moms.

From Personal to Public Change

Nearly 3 billion people of the world live on $2 a day or less, or an annual income of about $700, while one upper-middle-class home in the

United States uses as much total energy resources as a whole village in Bangladesh. Those who live on $2 a day roughly outnumber our U.S. population 10 to 1. Yet we control over 40 percent of the resources of this world. These 3 billion people are people much like us. They have many similar dreams and love their families as much as we do. What should be our response to this disequilibrium in our human family? The people and families described above illustrate a few concrete ways to live in the face of these unpleasant economic realities and the planet's limited ability to support life. Each of them withdrew from the illusory game of pretending control over their personal and collective futures in the name of a larger and more fascinating game.

I suppose you could say that the name of the game is "We're All in This Together." One of the principal mantras of this game is expressed in Aaron's words: we do it "because the world needs it." It is indeed, a very different game from the personal and collective game of consumption we are encouraged to play in the United States.

In our European and American culture we identify with great individuals. Our stories and our art, our plays and our movies and the history we write revolve around great heroes and heroines, great writers and poets, great soldiers, thinkers, and artists. This comes so naturally to us that when Lope de Vega in the play *Fuente Ovejuna* builds his narrative around a hero who turns out to be the entire village, which bears the name of the play, we are somewhat perplexed. But this cultural propensity puts us at a disadvantage, if we want to play the "all in it together" game. Yet it is the game of the twenty-first century, and it is indeed fascinating.

We are coming slowly to realize that we are a living part of a living organism that we have called the Earth, and the indigenous peoples of the world have called "Mother." In our time our "mother," on whom we depend for life, has been stressed to the breaking point by the actions of its human members. And it is the only mother we have. Even if we were to act decisively to change our behavior, it would not be sufficient if we acted alone. The new game calls us to find a way to use all of the wisdom and skill of the rich cultures that cradle the human members of this living Earth organism to save our mother and thereby save ourselves.

Slowly we are coming to realize that we, the people of the North, have become the unsustainable part of the human family and of the organism we call earth. Neither our rate of resource use nor our accumulation at the expense of other individuals and species can continue for long. If we continue with our game metaphor, the new game calls us to find a way to reverse undue accumulation of resources by this generation at the expense of our children's generations, and to reverse undue accumulation by small minorities at the expense of the majority of the human and non-human members of the organism. This, too, cannot be done acting alone. Nor will any of us survive and prosper for long unless we learn to play the "we're in it together" game well — and soon. In this twenty-first century there is a time limit on the game.

We have seen that the current economic system produces serious basic scarcities while at the same time channeling the fruit of the world's resources into increasingly fewer hands. These phenomena not only affect people of the "developing" countries. They affect us in the United States directly. A Bureau of Census study revealed that incomes for most of us are dropping in the United States. According to the study, real wages have dropped 3.6 percent from 2001 to 2004 while family indebtedness have risen 34 percent. At the same time, in the last thirty years the incomes of the richest 1 percent have risen 87 percent while those of the richest .01 percent have risen 497 percent.[4] And as we concentrate "wealth" in the hands of the few, we are at the same time literally consuming the world's capacity to provide for us. We must, so to speak, look for a new game. What might be some of the good "moves" we might make in the challenging game that is before us?

Here are some good moves we've seen people make.

- *Taking an immersion trip to poor communities in another country.* It's difficult to gain either the vision or the sense of urgency needed in our present situation without meeting first hand the people beyond our physical and ideological borders with whom we need to partner in this game in which the future of the planet is at stake. Some, like Samantha, have gone on immersion trips organized by their community or church, or by international organizations. (See a list of such organizations in appendix A.)

- *Finding a support community among friends and neighbors who share values and a fascination with the game.* We need the support and accompaniment of others as we make choices that run counter to the prevailing values around us.

- *Doing a disciplined reading of the signs of the times.* What is happening exactly? Why? Which groups have an interest that is being served by what is happening? How does the global situation impact the local and vice versa? We are all experts in our understanding of the reality around us, but we each see only one tiny "slice" of that reality. A reading of the signs of the times means an intentional effort to grow in awareness of what is happening beyond the borders of our personal experience. It also involves a commitment to find our own voice, our own statement about what needs to happen in the world of this time for which we were made. (The bilingual booklet *Reading the Signs of the Times/Interpretando los señales de los tiempos*[5] offers some suggestions that religion-based groups can use to do "sign reading").

- *Pushing ourselves to find alternative news sources.* Our reading of the signs of the times will reveal to us that commercial mass media provide us an extremely limited diet of "news" and consistently give this limited diet their own spin. We need to go out of our way to look for alternatives. You may have already discovered some of the following sources: Foreign Policy in Focus at *www.fpif.org, Sojourners Magazine,* The Americas Program at *www.americaspolicy.com, The Other Side,* Latin America Press, Maryknoll Office of Global Concerns — Newsnotes, and Common Dreams at *www.commondreams.org.* The Internet, in particular, offers many credible sources of alternative news and contact with newspapers from around the world (see appendix A for more suggestions).

- *Learning to know the cause, the interest, of minorities and of people who are poor.* We, like Greg Jaurequi, need to find a way to hear the voices of those working for change in the minority and poor communities. They will often break down deep-seated misperceptions about our common future together.

- *Finding ways to live more simply.* There is no way to resolve the abuse of our "mother" the earth without reducing our consumption in key areas. This is not primarily the responsibility of the poor but of those of us who are more affluent. Our resource use in the United States, for instance, exudes twenty-five tons of CO^2 per person annually into the atmosphere. The world average is three tons per person.

- *Once a week picking up a handful of soil and smelling it.* Let the "mother" remind us that we are indeed all in this together. Our fast-paced Western affluent society makes us forget that we are people of the earth and that we are dependent on it. Mixtec campesinos are very aware of this total dependence. It's harder for us city dwellers. We call ourselves "human" beings. Human reflects "humus," literally warm fertile soil.

These moves in the new game can suggest to us what our own original responses might be to the two primary challenges of the twenty-first century. But we must also make public, "political" choices in order to effect the changes of relationship between the members of the family of humanity and between our family and our Mother Earth.

New Community and Policy Moves in the United States

We are not strangers to this new spirit of solidarity, service, and hope that is called for. The spirit of the Mixtec peoples, of the movements and community work of the Latin American people, are part of our own history also, even though the dominant individualism and competitive corporate influence often makes us forget this fact.

My father-in-law, who grew up on the North Dakota prairies, used to tell stories about how the community of Norma, North Dakota, would harvest its wheat. At threshing time neighbors would plan together and form threshing crews to go from one farm to another, harvesting and threshing the wheat. Each farm prepared food and drinks for the crews, and then the crew would move on to the next farm until everyone had their wheat harvested. A clear form of North Dakota *gueza* that could be mistaken for a page from Mixtec history. He used to tell of the discussions that took place around the dinner table with the crews about the nature of the world and the politics of the Depression days. But threshing crews were not the only sign of a different vision of society in rural North Dakota. In the 1930s Dakotans, led by a farmers' populist movement headed by the "Non-Partisan League," chose to build a cooperative, non-corporate economy based upon cooperative grain terminals, flour mills, insurance companies, banks, electric coops, and gas stations, many of which form the backbone of the state economy today. Still today, North Dakota state law bans corporate-owned farms.

Given that history, it is not so surprising that North Dakotans recently stood up against the corporate powers of our day, represented in 2001 by the seed giant Monsanto, and banned genetically modified wheat in this state that produces 47 percent of U.S. wheat. According to Ted Nace writing in the May issue of *Orion* magazine, in 2004 Monsanto bowed to this pressure and withdrew all its pending applications for genetically modified Roundup Ready wheat. Dakotans know how to play the game of solidarity and community, the "we are all in this together game," with the same spirit as the Mixtecs of Tilantongo.

Even U.S. foreign policy history, in spite of its usual bellicose nature, contains examples of this other game. As the International Relations Center has pointed out recently, President Franklin Delano Roosevelt introduced in the 1930s his Good Neighbor policy, which reversed three decades of military interventions and racist stereotyping reminiscent of President Polk and the Mexican-American War. He committed the United States of that time to a different game, proclaiming, "I would dedicate this nation to the policy of the good neighbor — the neighbor who resolutely respects himself, and because he does so, respects the rights of others."[6] FDR recognized even then that we are all in this together, saying, "If I read the temper of our people correctly we now realize as we have never realized before our interdependence with each other — we cannot merely take but we must give as well."[7] In words that are similar to those of indigenous movements, campesino and student movements, and movements for an alternative type of globalization around the world, Roosevelt continued. We have learned "that we cannot live alone, at peace: that our own well-being is dependent on the well-being of other nations — far away. We have learned to be citizens of the world, members of the human community. We have learned the simple truth of Ralph Waldo Emerson that 'the only way to have a friend is to be one.' "[8]

On this basis the International Relations Center has put out a call to once again alter the course of U.S. foreign policy. They name it "A Global Good Neighbor Ethic for International Relations."[9]

In April, toward the end of the regular seven-month drought, members of the Zapotec indigenous people living around San Bartolo Coyotepec climb their sacred mountain to pray for rain. Community elders preside at the ritual, repeating aloud the names of the communities in their areas that will rely on the coming waters. After a pause last year, the presiding community elder added, "And we pray for rain not only for San Bartolo Coyotepec, we pray for rain for all of Oaxaca state and for all of the peoples of the world. We all belong to each other and to the earth and the fortune of one becomes the fortune of all."

Appendix A

Support and Information to Continue Learning

You'll find five categories of resources here. Immersion Trip Organizations, Credible News from Sources Independent of Large Media Corporations, Anti-Racism Resources, places where educated white people of good heart* can go to get grounded, and Action Groups. While we cluster these organizations according to these five categories, we wish to point out that considerable overlap exists between them. For example, an organization listed in the category of immersion trips may also provide credible alternative news, etc.

Immersion Trip Organizations

These represent a few organizations that offer quality cross-cultural and cross-class experiences. In addition to the following, many universities and language institutes offer similar trip experiences.

BorderLinks
www.borderlinks.org
    620 South Sixth Avenue
    Tucson, AZ 85701
    Tel.: 520-628-8263; Fax: 520-740-0242
    Caryn@borderlinks.org
Trip Experiences to the U.S.–Mexico Border

---

*The authors are educated white people, hopefully of good heart, so we do not use this term pejoratively but rather descriptively.

Community Links
www.commlinks.org
>   916 Wren Drive
>   San Jose, CA 95125
>   Tel./Fax: 408-723-5366
>   *peckos@comcast.net*

Trips offered to university, high school, and special interest groups.

Friends Across Borders
www.friendsacrossborders.org
>   Mission Awareness Trips Manager
>   P.O. Box 250710
>   Milwaukee, WI 53225
>   414-461-1810
>   *friendsacrossborders@mklm.org*

Trip experiences to Chile, Cambodia, Bolivia, El Salvador, U.S.–Mexico border, and East Africa sponsored by the Maryknoll Lay Missioners.

Global Awareness Through Experience
www.gate-travel.org/home.html
>   912 Market Street
>   LaCrosse, WI 54601
>   608-791-5283
>   *gate@fspa.org*

Trips to Mexico, Central America, Eastern Europe; programs for women.

Global Exchange–Reality Tours
www.globalexchange.org/tours/index.html
>   2017 Mission Street, #303
>   San Francisco, CA 94110
>   Tel.: 415-255-7296 Fax:: 415-255-7498

Trip experiences to about thirty destinations including U.S.–Mexico border, the Caribbean, Mexico, Central America, South America, Asia, Middle East, East Africa, and South Africa.

Ministry of Money
www.ministryofmoney.org/Pilgrimages_copy(1).htm
>   11315 Neelsville Church Road
>   Germantown, MD 20876
>   Tel.: 301-428-9560; Fax: 301-428-9573
>   *office@ministryofmoney.org*

Trips to Haiti, Gaza, Central America, Africa, and urban America.

Witness for Peace
www.witnessforpeace.org
>National Office
>3628 12th Street NE, 1st Floor
>Washington, DC 20017
>Tel.: 202-547-6112; Fax: 202-536-4708

Trips to Colombia, Cuba, Mexico, Nicaragua, Venezuela. Witness for Peace's mission is: "to support peace, justice and sustainable economies in the Americas by changing U.S. policies and corporate practices which contribute to poverty and oppression in Latin America and the Caribbean."

Credible News from Sources Independent of Large Media Corporations

American Friends Service Committee
www.afsc.org
>1501 Cherry Street
>Philadelphia, PA, 19102
>215-241-7000 (General Secretary)

Supported by the Quakers. Extensive information about Iraq, Immigrant Rights, Palestinian-Israeli Conflict, Africa: Life over Debt, Youth and Militarism, Economic Justice.

Americas Policy Watch
www.americaspolicy.org
www.ircamericas.org
>International Relations Center
>P.O. Box 2178
>Silver City NM 88062
>Tel.: 505-388-0208; Fax 505-388-0619
>*irc@irc-online.org*

The Americas Program of the International Resource Center is committed to improving hemispheric relations by advancing "a new world of citizen action, analysis, and policy options." Publishes regular policy briefs and an annual policy overview of U.S. foreign policy. In addition, it publishes two ezines, the *Boletín Transfronterizo* and the *Americas Updater,* as well as Citizen Action Profiles, which examines the successes and challenges of key citizen movements.

Center of Concern
www.coc.org
> 1225 Otis Street
> Washington, DC 20017
> Tel: 202-635-2757; Fax 202-832-9494
> *coc@coc.org*

The mission of the Center of Concern is grounded in shared religious social values and the challenges of Catholic social teaching. It emphasizes solidarity with those in poverty throughout the world. The Center's main focus is social justice and the transformation of inequitable structures and systems.

The work of the Center of Concern during the past several years has been directed at analyses of globalization through the lenses of gender, class, and race, with a concern for human rights, especially economic and social rights.

Working with a wide range of networks and coalitions, the Center contributes to international policy discussions and promotes people-centered economic development through education and advocacy. The Center reaches out to faith-based communities, churches, and schools; to grassroots groups and to other non-governmental organizations working for the common good; and to members of the international women's movement committed to justice for all women, their families and communities.

Common Dreams
www.commondreams.org
> P.O. Box 443
> Portland, ME 04112
> Tel: 207-775-0488; Fax: 207-775-0489
> *editor@commondreams.org*

"Common Dreams is a national nonprofit citizens' organization working to bring progressive Americans together to promote progressive visions for America's future. Founded in 1997, we are committed to being on the cutting-edge of using the Internet as a political organizing tool and creating new models for Internet activism." The web site presents "An eclectic mix of politics, issues, and breaking news with an emphasis on progressive perspectives that are increasingly hard to find with our corporate-dominated media."

CRISPAZ

www.crispaz.org
> 2 Lexington Street
> East Boston, MA 02128
> Tel.: 617-567-2900; Fax: 617-249-0769
> *info@crispaz.org*

"CRISPAZ, Christians for Peace in El Salvador, was founded in 1984. We are a faith-based organization dedicated to the mutual accompaniment with the church of the poor and marginalized communities in El Salvador. In building bridges of solidarity between communities in El Salvador and those in our home countries, we strive together for peace, justice, and human liberation. As an organization, we are politically nonpartisan and committed to nonviolence."

CRISPAZ provides volunteer opportunities, delegation trips to El Salvador, online shopping, and online news and publications.

Death Penalty Focus

www.deathpenalty.org
> 870 Market Street, Suite 859
> San Francisco, CA 94102
> Tel.: 415-243-0143; Fax: 415-243-0994
> *information@deathpenalty.org*

Founded in 1988, Death Penalty Focus is a nonprofit organization dedicated to the abolition of capital punishment through grassroots organizing, research, and the dissemination of information about the death penalty and its alternatives. Death Penalty Focus provides news and publications, speaker bureaus, forms for organizing against the death penalty, conferences, and the mobilization of demonstrations.

The Disarm Education Fund

www.disarm.org
> 113 University Place, 8th Floor
> New York, NY 10003
> Tel.: 212-353-9800; Fax: 212-353-9676

The Disarm Education Fund is a 501(c)(3) nonprofit that promotes peace, social justice, and human rights. Founded in 1976 as a gun-control group, DISARM has broadened its mission and been transformed into an internationally recognized advocacy and medical assistance organization.

Fellowship of Reconciliation / FOR
www.forusa.org
>521 North Broadway
>Nyack, NY 10960
>Tel.: 845-358-4601
>*for@forusa.org*

FOR seeks to replace violence, war, racism, and economic injustice with nonviolence, peace, and justice. We are an interfaith organization committed to active nonviolence as a transforming way of life and as a means of radical change. We educate, train, build coalitions, and engage in nonviolent and compassionate actions locally, nationally, and globally. The web site offers numerous possibilities and levels of participating in global peacemaking.

Foreign Policy in Focus (FPIF)
www.fpif.org
>Foreign Policy in Focus
>Institute for Policy Studies
>112 16th St. NW, Suite 600
>Washington, DC 20036
>Tel: (202) 234-9382
>*infocus@fpif.org*

Foreign Policy in Focus (FPIF) is a think tank for research, analysis, and action that brings together scholars, advocates, and activists who strive to make the United States a more responsible global partner. FPIF provides timely analysis of U.S. foreign policy and international affairs and recommends policy alternatives. We believe U.S. security and world stability are best advanced through a commitment to peace, justice, and environmental protection as well as economic, political, and social rights. We support diplomatic solutions, global cooperation, and grassroots participation as a guide for foreign policy.

FPIF publishes commentaries, briefs, and reports on its web site and organizes briefings for the public, media, lawmakers, and legislative staff. Staff and FPIF experts also write for newspapers, magazines, and other online publications and author books on foreign policy and international affairs. FPIF experts speak frequently on television and radio programs and are often quoted by print and online journalists.

International Development Exchange–IDEX
www.idex.org
> 827 Valencia Street, Suite 101
> San Francisco, CA 94110
> Tel.: 415-824-8384; Fax: 415-824-8387
> *info@idex.org*

IDEX is a San Francisco nonprofit organization that partners with grassroots groups in Africa, Asia, and Latin America, while actively engaging and educating North Americans in the challenges facing the communities in these regions. IDEX raises and distributes funds, builds alliances, and provides news and publications.

International Rivers
internationalrivers.org
> 1847 Berkeley Way
> Berkeley, CA 94703
> Tel.: 510-848-1155; Fax: 510-848-1008

International Rivers' (formerly International Rivers Network) mission is to protect rivers and defend the rights of communities that depend on them. International Rivers opposes destructive dams and the development model they advance, and encourages better ways of meeting people's needs for water and energy and protection from destructive floods. To achieve this mission, International Rivers collaborates with a global network of local communities, social movements, nongovernmental organizations and other partners. Through research, education, and advocacy, International Rivers works to halt destructive river infrastructure projects, to address the legacies of existing projects, improve development policies and practices, and to promote water and energy solutions for a just and sustainable world. The primary focus of International Rivers's work is in the global South.

Latin America Press / Noticias Aliadas
www.latinamericapress.org
> Apartado 18-0964, Lima 18, Peru
> Tel.: +511-265-9014 / 265-9098; Fax: +511-265-9186
> *postmaster@noticiasaliadas.org*

Noticias Aliadas is a nonprofit, nongovernmental organization based in Lima, Peru. We specialize in the production of information and analysis about events across Latin America and the Caribbean and have a network of correspondents based throughout the region. Last year we celebrated forty years of producing independent, reliable, and up-to-date information. The web site provides weekly in-depth information about citizens' movements in Latin America.

Maryknoll Office of Global Concerns
www.maryknollogc.org
> P.O. Box 29132
> Washington, DC 20017
> Tel.: 202-832-1780; Fax 202-832-5195
> *ogc@maryknoll.org*

Provides high quality information on issues regarding peace, ecology, economic justice, and social justice throughout Asia, Africa, and Latin America.

NETWORK
www.networklobby.org
> 25 E Street NW, Suite 200
> Washington, DC 20001
> Tel.: 202-347-9797; Fax: 202-347-9864
> *network@networklobby.org*

NETWORK is a Catholic leader in the global movement for justice and peace. It educates, lobbies, and organizes for economic and social transformation.

Nonviolence.org
www.nonviolence.org
> P.O. Box 38504
> Philadelphia, PA 19104
> *nvweb@nonviolence.org*

Nonviolence.org provides news and commentary from a pacifist perspective.

Ploughshares Fund
www.ploughshares.org
> Fort Mason Center
> Bldg. B, Suite 330
> San Francisco, CA 94123
> Tel.: 415-775-2244; Fax: 415-775-4529
> *ploughshares@ploughshares.org*

The Ploughshares Fund is a public grant-making foundation that supports initiatives to prevent the spread and use of nuclear, biological, and chemical weapons and other weapons of war, and to prevent conflicts that could lead to the use of weapons of mass destruction. The web site provides news and information on events in the foundation's area of expertise.

Project Underground
www.moles.org
> 1916A MLK Jr. Way
> Berkeley, CA 94704
> Tel.: 510-705-8981; Fax: 510-705-8983
> *project_underground@moles.org*

Project Underground exists as a vehicle for the environmental, human rights, and indigenous rights movements to carry out focused campaigns against abusive extractive resource activity. We seek to systematically deal with the problems created by the mining and oil industries by exposing environmental and human rights abuses by the corporations involved in these sectors and by building capacity among communities facing mineral and energy development to achieve economic and environmental justice.

Report on Guatemala
www.nisgua.org
> 1830 Connecticut Avenue NW
> Washington, DC 20009
> Tel.: 202-518-7638; Fax: 202-223-8221
> *info@nisgua.org*

NISGUA works for real democracy in Guatemala and the United States and strengthens the global movement for justice. NISGUA builds mutually beneficial grassroots ties between the people of the United States and Guatemala and advocates grassroots alternatives to challenge elite power structures and oppressive U.S. economic and foreign policy.

Resist, Inc.
www.resistinc.org
> 259 Elm Street
> Somerville, MA 02144
> 617-623-5110
> *resist@igc.org*

Resist, Inc., founded in 1967, provides funding, information, and resources to counter militarism in the United States, one of the most militarized countries in the world.

SIPAZ Report
www.sipaz.org
> Avenida Chilón #8
> Barrio El Cerrillo
> San Cristóbal de las Casas
> 29220 Chiapas, Mexico
> Tel./Fax: (+52.967) 63-160-55
> *chiapas@sipaz.org*

SIPAZ is a program of international observation that had its beginning in 1995, following the Zapatista uprising in 1994. It was formed to monitor the conflict in Chiapas, Mexico. Today SIPAZ supports the search for nonviolent solutions that contribute to the construction of a just peace through building tolerance and dialogue among the actors in Chiapas as well as, increasingly, in other areas in Mexico (Oaxaca and Guerrero). At the same time, SIPAZ serves as a bridge for communication and the sharing of information and experiences among organizations and networks that work toward the building of a just and lasting peace at local, national, regional, and international levels.

Teaching for Change
www.teachingforchange.org
> P.O. Box 73038
> Washington, DC 20056
> Tel.: 202-258-7204; Fax: 202-238-0109
> *info@teachingforchange.org*

Teaching for Change provides teachers and parents with the tools to transform schools into centers of justice where students learn to read, write, and change the world.

U.S./Labor Education in the Americas Project
www.usleap.org
> P.O. Box 268-290
> Chicago, IL 60626
> Tel.: 773-262-6502; Fax: 773-262-6602
> *apaul@usleap.org*

The U.S./Labor Education in the Americas Project (U.S./LEAP) works to support the basic rights of workers in Central America, Colombia,

Ecuador, and Mexico, especially those who are employed directly or indirectly by U.S. companies. Founded in 1987 as the U.S./Guatemala Labor Education Project (U.S./GLEP) by trade unionists and human rights advocates concerned about the basic rights of Guatemalan workers, U.S./LEAP has since expanded its work to other countries in the region. It works (1) to support worker justice in the global economy, specifically to support workers in Central America, Colombia, Ecuador, and Mexico who are fighting for dignity, respect, and justice; (2) to secure global rules for the global economy that ensure respect for the basic rights of workers; (3) to hold U.S. corporations responsible for worker rights' violations in the factories and on the plantations from which they buy in Central America, Colombia, Ecuador, and Mexico; (4) to support trade policies and programs that condition participation on respect for the basic rights of workers, and (5) to support the development of stronger cross-border relationships between Latin American workers and U.S. trade unions and community activists so that Latin America workers can more effectively use U.S. support campaigns to ensure their own rights.

Anti-Racism Organizations

Challenging White Supremacy
www.cwsworkshop.org
> CWS Workshop
> 2440 16th Street, PMB #275
> San Francisco, CA 94103
> 415-647-0921
> *cws@igc.org*

Challenging White Supremacy (CWS) workshop organizers believe that the most effective way to create fundamental social change in the United States is by building mass-based, multiracial grassroots movements led by radical activists of color. We also believe that the major barrier to creating these movements is racism or white supremacy. One way to challenge white supremacy is to do anti-racist training workshops in our own communities. CWS has worked in the broad-based radical, multiracial community of the Bay Area since 1993.

CWS workshops have been designed by a group of white anti-racist organizers. We believe our special responsibility is to help white social justice activists become principled and effective anti-racist organizers both to challenge our white privilege and to work for racial justice in all our social justice work.

Crossroads Ministry
www.crossroadsantiracism.org
> P.O. Box 309
> Matteson, IL 60443-0309
> Tel.: 708-503-0804; Fax 708-283-9491
> *info@crossroadsantiracism.org*

The mission of Crossroads Ministry is to dismantle systemic racism and build anti-racist, multicultural diversity within institutions and communities. This mission is implemented primarily by training institutional transformation teams and is guided by the following principles:

- The work of Crossroads is based upon a systemic analysis of racism and its individual, institutional, and cultural manifestations;
- The work of Crossroads is faith-based while at the same time non-sectarian, seeking to honor all expressions of spirituality that support and empower anti-racism;
- Crossroads seeks to be accountable in its work to those who share a common analysis of racism, and especially to communities of color;
- Crossroads understands its anti-racism work to be part of a national and global movement for racial justice and social equality;
- Crossroads recognizes that resistance to racism also requires resistance to all other forms of social inequality and oppression.

Where White, Educated People of Good Heart Can Go to Get Grounded

The following list comprises a few organizations where white, educated people who are seeking another perspective may go to meet kindred spirits or attend informational workshops or transformational retreats well suited to provide ongoing input to formulating a different worldview and life stance.

Center for Action and Contemplation
www.cacradicalgrace.org
> P.O. Box 12464
> Albuquerque, NM 87195
> 505-242-9588
> *info@cacradicalgrace.org*

Center for Action and Contemplation supports a new reformation — From the inside!

* In the spirit of the Gospels
* Confirming people's deeper spiritual intuitions
* Encouraging actions of justice rooted in prayer
* With a new appreciation for, and cooperation with, other denominations, religions, and cultures

Offers retreats and print and web-based information and events. Also offers a program directed specifically to men: *www.malespirituality.org.*

JustFaith
www.justfaith.org
    JustFaith Ministries
    P.O. Box 221348
    Louisville, KY 40252
    Tel.: 502-429-0865; Fax: 502-429-0897
    info@justfaith.org
JustFaith Ministries strives to provide faith formation processes and resources that emphasize the Gospel message of peace and justice, Catholic social teaching, and the intersection of spirituality and action. The aim of JustFaith Ministries is to enable people of faith to develop a passion for justice and to express this passion in concrete acts of social ministry.

Maryknoll Affiliates
www.maryknoll.org/MARYKNOLL/AFFILIATES
    3600 South Seeley Avenue
    Chicago, IL 60609
    773-927-9257
    inquiry@maryknollaffiliates.org
Maryknoll Affiliates comprises small communities of people distributed throughout the United States, the Philippines, Nicaragua, Puerto Rico, and Peru oriented by spirituality, a global vision, community, and action. These groups generally follow the vision of the Maryknoll Missioners, a Roman Catholic global mission organization dedicated to mission work reflecting cultural sensitivity and work to promote peace and justice.

Mexican American Cultural Center
www.maccsa.org
    3115 West Ashby Place
    P.O. Box 28185
    San Antonio, TX 78228
    Tel.: 210-732-2156; Fax: 210-732-9072
    register@maccsa.org
The Mexican American Cultural Center empowers and educates leaders for service in a culturally diverse church and society. It provides a bookstore, courses, and workshops at its San Antonio Center.

Pace e Bene
paceebene.org
    2501 Harrison Street
    Oakland, CA 94612
    510-268-8765
    info@paceebene.org
Pace e Bene's mission is to develop the spirituality and practice of active nonviolence as a way of living and being and as a process for cultural transformation. It provides training, news, publications, and events supporting nonviolent options.

Action Groups

There are thousands of not-for-profit organizations carrying out professional works sustained by a passion for the creation and promotion of a dominant worldview more consistent with a desire to pass along a healthy planet to our grandchildren. We list two here that we know well:

Maryknoll Lay Missioners
www.laymissioners.maryknoll.org
    P.O. Box 307
    Maryknoll, NY 10545
    914-762-6364
    info@mklm.org
Maryknoll Lay Missioners is a Catholic organization inspired by the mission of Jesus to live and work with poor communities in Africa, Asia, and the Americas, responding to basic needs and helping to create a more just and compassionate world.

Mexico Solidarity and Action Fund – MESA
www.mesamexico.org
info@mesamexico.org
The two authors participate in this collective effort in Mexico by Maryknoll Lay Missioners to build self-reliance and self-esteem through programs in health, community economics, environment and agriculture, formation and human rights, and migration among the indigenous and poor of Oaxaca and Querétaro states in Mexico.

Appendix B

Citizen Declarations

We have included four statements by citizens' movements and indigenous leaders to give a sense of the vision and convictions of movements for an alternative vision of our common future.

Declaration of the People of Oaxaca

This statement was collectively drafted in August of 2006 by the citizens' movement of Oaxaca state called the Popular Assembly of the Peoples of Oaxaca, a coalition that continues to work for the removal of a corrupt and repressive state governor and for the long-term goal of statewide governmental reform.

The People of Oaxaca live difficult times. Nevertheless, these are not new times for us. For several years now the increasing political violence, the ongoing violation of human rights, and the wave of murders of women have deeply concerned and saddened us. In response to innumerable problems and before the people's demands for justice, the situation grows ever more severe with the silence, inaction, indifference, and impunity of the state government, which makes it directly responsible for the situation of ingovernability in the state.

The people of Oaxaca grow in awareness and understanding. We hear the cries of indignation of the multitudes who have marched in our streets. The straw that broke the camel's back to fully reveal the blunt reality of this regime's authoritarianism was the recent government action of June 14, during which it employed its security forces irrationally. We can no longer remain silent, and we want solutions for Oaxaca's problems.

We reject the government of Ulises Ruiz Ortiz, because we do not accept a government that uses public resources to benefit only one privileged sector of society. We withdraw our support for institutions that do not fulfill their obligations and are used to silence the voice of the people in order to benefit political parties. We are fed up with empty speeches full of lies.

These words arise from our living memory of acts and aggression against us committed in order to maintain the power of those who govern us and who benefit from total impunity.

Let's remember together:

Starting in 2004, we have had to endure murders that were really political assassinations with cover-ups. Since then, human rights violations have been constant, our right to free speech has been repressed; independent union activity has been curtailed, and in the rural areas of the state, local fiefdoms have been strengthened to benefit political interests. Justice has been applied both capriciously and in a biased way. Police forces charged with enforcing the law have been converted into tools to enforce the power of those who repress political opposition and the local leaders of the people.

We've heard hundreds of times that the state of Oaxaca is one of the richest regions of the country in cultural and environmental diversity. Nevertheless, no policies exist that recognize and support efforts by indigenous peoples as they relate with their natural resources and environment in ways that both preserve the health of the environment as well as contribute to the people's development. Government programs, on the contrary, have reduced production in the rural zones, damaged the environment, and marginalized the indigenous people. This situation creates the necessity for emigration, opening the door for the government to grant concessions of vital resources, such as water, to the benefit of transnational corporations.

Institutions responsible for public health do not carry out their functions. They are too slow to provide urgent care for serious diseases such as cervical and uterine cancer, and we are experiencing an alarming increase in maternal mortality. Public hospitals do not have sufficient medicine on hand, and they lack the minimum requirements of medical equipment. Education in our state suffers similar deficiencies not only in terms of inadequate budgets but also in content and educational perspective. At the same time, the government wastes public funds on unnecessary and damaging projects like the "remodeling" of the historic zone of our city, in effect an assault on the cultural patrimony of Oaxacans.

The government maintains secrecy regarding its actions and public expenditures. Public projects are clandestinely awarded to businesses operated by family members and close friends of the governor. And then, to add insult to injury, both state and federal social programs are utilized by the state government, not to provide public services but rather to forward its own party and political self-interests.

The government assaults our traditions. It commercializes our culture in brutish ways, insulting our population, and it openly interferes in municipalities and villages that do not bow to its interests. At the same time, it creates both confusion and violence in our indigenous communities who legally choose to elect their leaders according to traditional norms and who follow their cultural traditions. The government denies the people's preferences as it imposes municipal administrators charged to fracture communal unity in our indigenous communities.

All of this offers ample evidence that we are living in a situation of de facto martial law. And for this reason, the people of Oaxaca unite together, not only to demand political justice and to revoke the governor's mandate but also to lay the foundation for governments that will represent us in the future.

We want and need a true government, a government that represents the people of Oaxaca in all of its diversity: indigenous peoples, urban population, rural farm workers, workers, business executives, women, men, children, youth, gay and lesbian. A government whose priority activity is to establish dialogue and works to hear everyone's voice; that establishes public institutions, policies, and laws that accord with the cultural diversity and autonomy of the peoples and communities of Oaxaca; that respects freedom of speech and foments communications media reflecting the plurality of our cultures. A government that generates participation of the citizens in order to create development, democracy, and stability in the state. A government that actively seeks solutions to the political, social, and economic problems of Oaxaca and works to create institutions that represent the people and operate transparently in reporting on their expenditures and thus fulfilling the will of the people they serve.

In order to build this new form of government, we are creating a Program for Political Unity; we call for a new pact based upon the dialogue of all of the sectors of the people of Oaxaca. Together, we will build new political channels that will respect human rights; that will respect the communal life of indigenous peoples and the autonomy of our municipalities; that will generate equality, equity, and transparency. Most of all, we call for the reestablishment of a state based on constitutional rights, on democracy and political stability through the creation of a new constitution for our state, to reflect the voices and the desires of the Oaxacan people.

This "Declaration of the People of Oaxaca" is an open document focusing on the desires and demands of men and women, of campesinos, of indigenous communities and peoples, of business people, independent unions, workers, teachers, students and professionals, of people with different capacities, of people of all faith traditions and religious thought, of people from diverse sexual orientations and of all those who believe that it is possible not only to dream of a better Oaxaca, but are also willing to work together to build a more just society and a government that truly represents us and works for and with us to make Oaxaca as it should be: a land in which we can live with dignity and justice.

Oaxaca de Juárez, Agosto de 2006

Statement by Chief Joseph, Indigenous Leader of the Nez Percé Peoples to U.S. Government Leaders, Washington, DC, 1879

At last I was granted permission to come to Washington and bring my friend Yellow Bull and our interpreter with me. I am glad I came. I have shaken hands with a good many friends, but there are some things I want to know which no one seems able to explain. I cannot understand how the government sends a man out to fight us, as it did General Miles, and then breaks his word. Such a government has something wrong about it. I cannot understand why so many chiefs are allowed to talk so many different ways, and promise so many different things. I have seen the Great Father Chief [President Hayes]; the Next Great Chief [Secretary of the Interior]; the Commissioner Chief; the Law Chief; and many other law chiefs [Congressmen] and they all say they are my friends, and that I shall have justice, but while all their mouths talk right I do not understand why nothing is done for my people. I have heard talk and talk but nothing is done. Good words do not last long unless they amount to something. Words do not pay for my dead people. They do not pay for my country now overrun by white men. They do not protect my father's grave. They do not pay for my horses and cattle. Good words do not

Text: Chester Anders Fee, *Chief Joseph: The Biography of a Great Indian* (New York: Wilson-Erickson, 1936).

give me back my children. Good words will not make good the promise of your war chief, General Miles. Good words will not give my people a home where they can live in peace and take care of themselves. I am tired of talk that comes to nothing. It makes my heart sick when I remember all the good words and all the broken promises. There has been too much talking by men who had no right to talk. Too many misinterpretations have been made; too many misunderstandings have come up between the white men and the Indians. If the white man wants to live in peace with the Indian he can live in peace. There need be no trouble. Treat all men alike. Give them the same laws. Give them all an even chance to live and grow. All men were made by the same Great Spirit Chief. They are all brothers. The earth is the mother of all people, and all people should have equal rights upon it. You might as well expect all rivers to run backward as that any man who was born a free man should be contented penned up and denied liberty to go where he pleases. If you tie a horse to a stake, do you expect he will grow fat? If you pen an Indian up on a small spot of earth and compel him to stay there, he will not be contented nor will he grow and prosper. I have asked some of the Great White Chiefs where they get their authority to say to the Indian that he shall stay in one place, while he sees white men going where they please. They cannot tell me.

I only ask of the Government to be treated as all other men are treated. If I cannot go to my own home, let me have a home in a country where my people will not die so fast. I would like to go to Bitter Root Valley. There my people would be happy; where they are now they are dying. Three have died since I left my camp to come to Washington.

When I think of our condition, my heart is heavy. I see men of my own race treated as outlaws and driven from country to country, or shot down like animals.

I know that my race must change. We cannot hold our own with the white men as we are. We only ask an even chance to live as other men live. We ask to be recognized as men. We ask that the same law shall work alike on all men. If an Indian breaks the law, punish him by the law. If a white man breaks the law, punish him also.

Let me be a free man, free to travel, free to stop, free to work, free to trade where I choose, free to choose my own teachers, free to follow the religion of my fathers, free to talk, think, and act for myself — and I will obey every law or submit to the penalty.

Whenever the white man treats the Indian as they treat each other then we shall have no more wars. We shall be all alike — brothers of one father and mother, with one sky above us and one country around us and one government for all. Then the Great Spirit Chief who rules above will smile upon this land and send rain to wash out the bloody spots made by brothers' hands upon the face of the earth. For this time the Indian race is waiting and praying. I hope no more groans of wounded men and women will ever go to the ear of the Great Spirit Chief above, and that all people may be one people.

Hin-mah-too-yah-lat-kekht has spoken for his people.

U.S.–Mexico Binational Family Farmer and Farmworker Congress Final Declaration Mexico City, September 28, 2006

We the undersigned participants in the Binational Congress of Campesinos, Indigenous Peoples, Family Farmers and Migrant Farm Workers declare our unity in defending our rights to continue working on the land.

We affirm that the principle of food sovereignty is the basis for an agricultural system that is healthy, sustainable, and just. Food Sovereignty is the right of the peoples and nations to define their own agricultural and trade policies, in which small family producers, campesinos, and indigenous peoples play a fundamental role. We demand laws and domestic agricultural policies that do not impact on domestic markets of neighboring countries.

We demand a fair trade of agricultural products that respects the viability of neighboring national markets. That is why we oppose the free trade agreements that facilitate and legalize the invasion of products at prices below the cost of production and that prioritize transnational export and agribusiness corporations. In particular, we oppose the policies and agreements contained in the WTO, NAFTA, CAFTA-DR and other bilateral free-trade agreements. Given the profound crisis in the countryside, we demand that the WTO, NAFTA, and all other trade agreements get out of agriculture, because they are an attack on people's well-being and democratic processes, and trump agricultural policies that support rural and family economies.

In 2008, the completion of the opening of the U.S., Canadian, and Mexican markets under NAFTA is set to occur, which would mean the deepening of the farm crisis in all three countries, and as a result, the displacement of thousands of campesino and indigenous peoples from their places of origin and, in the United States, the near completion of the disappearance of family farms. For this reason, we demand that the agricultural chapter of NAFTA be eliminated, as a means of assuring the survival of producers from both sides of the border.

We think that among the principal causes of the high levels of migration is the concentration of economic and political power in the hands of large transnational corporations and the policies that favor them, especially in the agricultural sector. The massive exodus from the Mexican and Central American countryside is largely a result of the trade and agricultural policies already mentioned.

We support movement in favor of immigrant rights in the United States, including a comprehensive immigration reform, with paths to legalization and citizenship for migrants. We demand humane and dignified treatment for farm workers who come to Mexico from Central America. They are our neighbors, our sisters and brothers. In the long term, the only solution to the problem of mass forced migration is a profound change in the economic model, in North America and worldwide. We demand the demilitarization of the border and the destruction of the walls that have caused so many tragic deaths in the border region. We have a vision of an economic model that does not force people to migrate because of precarious economic conditions.

We believe that a deep reform of the 2007 Farm Bill in the United States is a matter of great urgency. We want an agricultural law that makes it possible for farmers to receive a fair price, guaranteeing a minimum price above the costs of production. To achieve this there must be a reduction in overproduction, by means of supply management programs, of conservation programs, and through commodity reserves controlled by family farmers. We want anti-trust laws — which have been largely ignored in recent decades — to be enforced, in order to diminish the dangerous control by agribusiness of the agricultural markets.

We recognize that there is a crisis of land loss among African Americans, Indigenous, Asian Americans, Latinos and women, and we demand an end to discrimination to assure full access to land, to credits, and to all the necessary federal agricultural programs.

The economic policies directed to the Mexican countryside are generating rejection by the population, as is being manifested in Oaxaca. This Binational Congress of Small and Campesino Farmers expresses our solidarity with the teacher and popular movement headed by the Popular Assembly of the Peoples of Oaxaca (APPO), whose principal demand is the departure of the current governor of the state, Mr. Ulises

Ruiz. We will maintain our vigilance over the situation in Oaxaca and we emphatically reject any resolution of the conflict by force.

We support the worldview of the indigenous peoples who have shown us that the basic elements of life, such as land, water, air, and seeds, must be accessible to everyone. The concentration of these elements in few privileged and powerful hands threatens the future of humanity. In particular, genetically modified seeds are a threat against biodiversity and the rights of farmers to conserve varieties of seeds, plants, and animals that have nourished humanity for millennia. We support the right of indigenous peoples to collective control of their territories and of biodiversity.

The undersigned,

Rural Coalition/Coalición Rural, *Washington, DC, and Mexico City*

Federation of Southern Cooperatives/Land Assistance Fund, *Atlanta, GA*

Friends of the Earth USA, *Washington, DC*

National Family Farm Coalition, *Washington, DC*

Maryknoll Office of Global Concerns, *Washington DC*

Via Campesina North American Region

Border Agricultural Workers Project, *El Paso, TX*

Family Farm Defenders, *Madison, WI*

Farmworker Association of Florida, *Apopka, FL*

Organización de Líderes Campesinas de California, *Pomona, CA*

Agriculture Missions, Inc., *New York, NY*

Hispanic Organizations Leadership Alliance, *Takoma Park, MD*

National Latino Farmers and Ranchers Trade Association, *Takoma Park, MD*

Texas-Mexico Border Coalition, *Texas*

Centro de Desarrollo Integral Campesino de la Mixteca (CEDICAM), *Oaxaca*

Frente Democrático Campesino de Chihuahua

Servicios del Pueblo Mixe–Ser Mixe, *Oaxaca*

Unión de Organizaciones de la Sierra Juárez de Oaxaca (UNOSJO)

Organización de Agricultores Biológicos de Oaxaca (ORAB)

Kie' Lui, *Oaxaca*

Promotores de Salud (PROSA), *Oaxaca*

Unión Nacional de Organizaciones Regionales Autónomos (UNORCA), *Mexico City*

Asociación de Empresas Comercializadoras del Campo (ANEC), *Mexico City*

Grupo Vicente Guerrero, *Tlaxcala*

Servicios para una Educación Alternativa (EDUCA), *Oaxaca*

Universidad Autónoma Metropolitana, *Mexico City*

Promotores Campesinos Conservacionistas

Centro de Estudios para el Cambio en el Campo (CECCAM), *Mexico City*

Organización Regional Nahuatl Independiente (ORNI), *Puebla*

NETECO, *Puebla*

Centro de Estudios para el Desarrollo Rural (CESDER), *Puebla*

Declaration of the Fourth Mesoamerican Forum
Tegucigalpa, Honduras
July 21–24, 2003

The Fourth Mesoamerican Forum "For the Self-determination and Resistance of the Peoples of Mesoamerica," declares that:

- Privatization of public services has generally brought higher prices, and the resulting consolidation of private monopolies and oligopolies providing public services has stimulated corruption while undermining the cultures and the sovereignty of the peoples of Mesoamerica. *We believe that access to public services is a basic human right, and we categorically reject the notion that these services are "merchandise" and should be subject to market forces.*

- Free trade agreements, the Plan Puebla Panama, and the Free Trade Area of the Americas all promote a foreign investment strategy based on assembly plant (*maquiladora*) production the goal of which is a "flexible workforce" and the exploitation of workers — especially women. *We oppose this competition to reduce labor costs and make the lives of workers more precarious. We demand that workers' rights be protected by strong national employment policies and programs that create decent jobs.*

- Mesoamerica is one of the regions of the planet richest in biodiversity. This wealth makes it an area of enormous interest to transnational businesses involved in bio-prospecting. Armed with expanding intellectual property rights, these businesses threaten to sack the rich array of animal and plant species of our countries. These foreign corporations also steal and patent the traditional knowledge of our indigenous peoples and use foreign investment, backed by the investment chapters of free trade agreements, to violate our environmental laws. *We therefore reject agreements on intellectual property rights and on investments that legitimize bio-piracy in Mesoamerica.*

- *We denounce the repression of indigenous communities and communities of Afro descent that projects such as the Plan Puebla Panama and commercial treaties promote. Through privatization programs and dam and highway construction projects, they dispossess these communities of lands to which they have legitimate rights, seriously harming the interests of these sectors of our populations.*

- Neo-liberal policies and reforms have provoked the destruction of campesino agriculture in Mesoamerica and deepened rural poverty. These policies have also led to the reconcentration of land in the hands of the few, creating an agricultural counterreform. *We reject the anti-agricultural slant of the present economic policies and the abandonment of the rural sector by government programs. We reject the production of genetically modified foods and the loss of food sovereignty by the peoples of the region. All of these problems will be aggravated by free trade agreements between Central America and the United States. Such agreements will leave intact non-trade barriers such as health and sanitation regulations, which will be used to block entrance of Central American products to the United States. This, along with continued subsidies for the agricultural sector of the United States, will convert the economies of Mesoamerica into importers of U.S. production, and these economies will lose their own productive capacity.*

- Free trade agreements take away from Central American nations the tools that would permit the implementation of effective national development strategies. They prevent the establishment of competitive national production networks and regulations to assure foreign investment promotes real development. *We favor national development projects based on democratic and sustainable principles that reduce our deep gender, ethnic, social, and geographic inequalities.*

- We recognize that constructing viable alternatives in Mesoamerica will require systems of economic solidarity serving real human needs through production and marketing networks and community services provided by organized communities and an empowered population. *We support national development projects that generate opportunities for all and that contribute to containing national and international migratory flows.*

- We believe that the strategies of the free trade agreements and the FTAA are neither the only nor the best strategies to guarantee international economic participation for our countries. *We emphatically reject free trade strategies that serve primarily to facilitate capital accumulation by transnational companies and whose logic violates the most elemental human rights. We advocate an authentic people-centered economic integration project founded on comprehensive economic, social, environmental, cultural, technical, and energy agreements.*

- *We propose the demilitarization of our countries and the immediate withdrawal of U.S. military bases in the region, and we advocate the immediate elimination of national armies and military budgets so that these funds can be used for social development.*

Another Mesoamerica is possible!

For the self-determination and resistance of the peoples of Mesoamerica!

Notes

Preface

1. Statistical Abstract of the United States, 2007, Table #671, Figure from 2004, *www.census.gov/compendia/statab/*.

Invitation

1. James Polk, quoted in Francisco Martín Moreno, *México mutilado* (Miami: Alfaguara/Santillana USA, 2004).

2. Ecological Footprint of Nations 2005 Update, Dr. Jason Venetoulis and Dr. John Talbert, sponsored by Redefining Progress/Ecological Footprint. See online *www.ecologicalfootprint.org/pdf/Footprint%20of%20Nations%202005.pdf*. These sophisticated land use studies concluded that we can achieve global sustainability provided that on the average, each person in the world consumed the product of 15.71 hectares annually. As of 2005, the United States per capita consumption was 108.95 or 6.93 times the estimated sustainable rate. See also *www.ecologicalfootprint.org* and *www.myfootprint.org/* and World Wildlife Fund's 2006 Living Planet Report.

2. Cultural Genetics

1. The Native Plant Society can be found at *http://aznps.org/*.

2. Teocintle, or Teocinte (*Zea mays ssp Mexicana*), still occurs naturally in some parts of Mexico.

3. *Milpa* is the word commonly used for a field of corn, but more accurately a field of the traditional companion plants, corn, beans, and squash, which have been the staples of the Mexican diet for centuries.

4. GM seeds are produced by laboratory processes that modify plant and animal genes in ways not possible in nature. Some introduce genetic material to seeds that make them resistant to herbicides, others to certain insects. These modifications are patented, so that if they should pass to normal seeds, these seeds then fall under the manufacturer's patent.

5. See Ignacio Chapela and David Quist, "Transgenic DNA Introgressed into Traditional Maize Landraces in Oaxaca, Mexico," *Nature Magazine,* November 29, 2001. Chapela describes the first known case of crossing of GM corn with native varieties in the Sierra Juárez of the state of Oaxaca, Mexico.

6. See the Center for Food Safety, *Monsanto vs. U.S. Farmers Report,* 2005, 15, *www.centerforfoodsafety.org/Monsantovsusfarmersreport.cfm*.

7. Thomas Berry, *The Dream of the Earth* (San Francisco: Sierra Club Books, 1988).

8. Ibid., 93.

9. Ronald C. Kessler et al., "Lifetime Prevalence and Age-of-Onset Distributions of DSM-IV Disorders in the National Comorbidity Survey Replication," *Archives of General Psychiatry* 62 (2005): 593–602. *http://archpsyc.ama-assn.org/cgi/content/full/62/6/593.*

10. For more information on U.S. interventions against democratically elected governments or democratic popular movements, see Greg Grandin, *Empire's Workshop: Latin America, the United States, and the Rise of the New Imperialism* (New York: Metropolitan Books, 2006).

11. For more on these effects of the "green revolution," see Angus Wright, *The Death of Ramón González* (Austin: University of Texas Press, 2005); Peter Rosset, "Gateses' Approach to Hunger Is Bound to Fail," *Seattle Post-Intelligencer,* September 22, 2006.

3. A Glimpse into the Mixtec World

1. *Presencias de la cultura mixteca* (Huajuapan de León, Oaxaca: Universidad Tecnológica de la Mixteca, 2001), 21–30.

2. María de Los Angeles Ojeda and Cecilia Rossell, *Las mujeres y sus diosas en los códices prehispánicos de Oaxaca* (Mexico City: CIESAS, 2003).

3. María de Los Angeles Romero Frizzi, *Economía y vida de los españoles en la Mixteca Alta: 1519–1720* (Mexico City: Instituto Nacional de Antropología e Historia, 1990).

4. Angus Wright, *The Death of Ramón González* (Austin: University of Texas Press, 2005), 164.

5. There are no corresponding words in Spanish or English since there are no social phenomena that exactly correspond in our two cultures. See glossary.

6. *Presencias de la cultura mixteca,* 62–65.

4. A Mixtec Teaching about Work

1. Thomas Berry, *The Great Work: Our Way into the Future* (New York: Bell Tower, 1999).

2. Laurette Séjourné, *El universo de Quetzalcóatl* (Mexico City: Fondo de Cultura Económica, 1994).

3. Ibid.

4. Kofi Anan, a Ghanaian-born diplomat, served as the seventh secretary general of the United Nations from 1997 to 2006.

5. In 1886, the Federation of Organized Trades and Labor Unions called for a U.S. labor movement to achieve a standard eight-hour work day, instead of ten, twelve, even sixteen hours. On May 1, 1886, a bomb was thrown at police in a Chicago demonstration resulting in chaotic gunfire killing several police and demonstrators. Seven men were later convicted in a grossly unfair trial as they were never linked with the bomb thrower and some were not even present at the demonstration. Four were hanged; one committed apparent suicide; two were pardoned. These were the Haymarket Riot martyrs.

6. See the text of "Everyday Low Wages: The Hidden Price We All Pay for Wal-Mart," Wal-Mart's Labor Record submitted by Congressman George Miller, Democratic staff of the Committee on Education and the Workforce, U.S. House of Representatives: *www.mindfully.org/Industry/2004/Wal-Mart-Labor-Record16feb04.htm.*

7. Institute for Local Self-Reliance, *The Economic Impact of Locally Owned Businesses vs. Chains: A Case Study in Midcoast Maine* (Minneapolis, 2003). Don Houston, *Civic Economics, Economic Impact Analysis, A Case Study: Local Merchants vs. Chain Retailers* (LivableCity Austin, December 2002), yielded results of $45 returned to the local community from $100 spent at a local business, $13 returned to the community from the same $100 spent at a national chain store.

8. *http://pubdb3.census.gov/macro/032005/hhinc/new05_000.htm.*

9. Jim Wallis, *God's Politics: Why the Right Gets It Wrong and the Left Doesn't Get It* (New York: HarperCollins, 2005), 279.

10. Brian Swimme in an article published in *US Catholic,* June 1997, says that "the average three-year-old in America is taking in 10,000 advertisements a year."

11. According to New American Dream: "More than 100 million trees' worth of bulk mail arrive in American mail boxes each year — that's the equivalent of deforesting the entire Rocky Mountain National Park every four months." Online see *www.newdream.org/Junkmail/facts.php/.*

12. Tom Barry et al., *A Global Good Neighbor Ethic for International Relations,* International Relations Center/Foreign Policy in Focus Special Report, May 2005, *www.irc-online.org/content/ggn/0505ggn.php.*

13. For more information on the genocide committed against indigenous villages under the presidency of Guatemala's Ríos Montt, see Thomas A. Melville, *Through a Glass Darkly: The U.S. Holocaust in Central America* (Philadelphia: XLibris, 2005).

5. Money, Wealth, and Mixtec Fiestas

1. See David Korton, "Money vs. Wealth," at *www.ratical.org/many_worlds/cc/Korten.html.* Korten cites William Greider, *One World, Ready or Not* (New York: Simon and Schuster, 1997), 232. For further discussion of the problem of capital market liberalization and the turn to speculative investment see Joseph Stiglitz, "The Roaring Nineties," *Atlantic Monthly,* October 2002.

2. Figures for 2002. According to EarthTrends, World Resources Institute, *www.wri.org,* as of April 22, 2007.

3. The fact is that some of the richest individuals in the world, for example, Carlos Slim, are Mexican and came by their riches partly thanks to the advantages of "free trade" and market liberalization.

4. Jared Diamond, *Collapse: How Societies Choose to Fail or Succeed* (New York: Viking Books, 2005), 158.

5. From conversations with researchers at Iowa State University regarding their investigations in San Miguel Jaltepec in the Mixteca Alta.

6. For details on these various corn-based dishes see the glossary.

7. For an account of the Rockefeller Foundation's role in promoting this agricultural "revolution" starting in northern Mexico see Angus Wright, *The Death of Ramón González* (Austin: University of Texas Press, 2005).

8. For more on the process of genetic engineering of seeds and how this differs from hybridization see Mateo Miguel García, special report, "¿Qué son los organismos geneticamente modificado?" in *El Consumidor.*

9. There are more direct ways to create competitive scarcity. The United States, in the early stages of the occupation of Iraq, imposed economic reforms that, among other things, prohibited Iraqi farmers, who live in an area thought to be the birthplace of Western agriculture, "from saving heirloom seeds from one year to the next, obliging them to buy them anew each season from corporations like Monsanto and Dow Chemical" (*Empire's Workshop*, 160–61).

10. For a fuller description see Grandin, *Empire's Workshop.*

11. In early 2007 corn prices suddenly rose in Mexico, followed by further huge increases in the price of tortillas and all corn-dependent products such as eggs, milk, meat, and poultry. Faced with international corporations using hoarding to provoke scarcity and a resultant increase in the price of corn, and using this price increase as an excuse for unconscionable hikes in food prices, the Mexican government has found itself stripped by free trade regulations of any tools for controlling price excesses in the same way it was at the mercy of low corn prices earlier.

12. See also the video documentary *An Inconvenient Truth,* produced by former Vice President Al Gore, *www.climatecrisis.net.*

13. Trade and globalization, as economist Joseph Stiglitz continues to point out, does not have to function this way. See Joseph E. Stiglitz, *Globalization and Its Discontents* (New York: W. W. Norton, 2002). See also Peter Rosset, *Food Is Different: Why the WTO Should Get Out of Agriculture* (New York: Palgrave Macmillan, 2006), to understand better why the open markets created by the current brand of free trade benefit U.S. firms much more than they do the developing countries who sign on.

14. On the increasing gap between the rich and the poor in the United States see Jared Bernstein, Elizabeth McNichol, and Karen Lyons, *Pulling Apart: A State-by-State Analysis of Income Trends,* published by the Center on Budget and Policy Priorities and the Economic Policy Institute, January 2006. Available at *www.epinet.org/studies/pulling06/pulling_apart_2006.pdf.* José Antonio Ocampo, director of the Economic Commission for Latin America, in May of 2003 stated that the relative poverty levels in Latin America continued higher than those in 1980. He continues, "Since per capita income is slightly higher than in 1980, this is an unequivocal sign of the decline in distribution over the past two decades" (*La Jornada de México,* May 8, 2003, 5).

15. *La Jornada de México,* April 18, 2006, 34. Since 1980 Latin America's gross regional product, under liberalized markets and privatization strategies, has diminished by $2.6 trillion and in the last seven years it has made a net transfer of wealth to the North of $200 billion in loan payments. International Monetary Fund figures (*La Jornada de México,* April 19, 2006).

16. Presentations at Water Forum, "Foro de Experiencias y Alternativas de Uso y Manejo del Agua," February 23–24, 2006, Autonomous University of Mexico, Mexico City. For a more detailed analysis of the issue of water privatization, see Maude Barlow, "Water as a Commodity," *Food First Backgrounder* 7, no. 3 (Summer 2001), Institute for Food and Development Policy; see also Heinrich Boll Foundation, Global Issues Paper no. 5, *Grab for Water.*

17. Center for Multidisciplinary Analysis, Economics Faculty, Autonomous University of Mexico, reported by Patricia Muñoz Ríos, "El poder adquisitivo ha caído en los tres sexenios recientes," *La Jornada de México,* March 27, 2006.

18. Enrique Galván Ochoa, in his column, "Dinero," *La Jornada de México.*

19. Instituto Nacional de Estadística, Geografía e Informática, Juan Antonio Zuñiga, "INEGI: Hay casi un millón 550 mil personas desocupadas en México," *La Jornada de México,* May 17, 2006.

20. According to interviews with Oaxacan farmers.

6. Objection!

1. The Human Development Index reveals that many of Mexico's poorest municipalities compare with conditions in sub-Sarahan Africa, the poorest zone on earth. See *http://hdr.undp.org* and at the Oaxaca state government's web site under Estado > Fichas Municipales, currently at *www.e-oaxaca.gob.mx/web/index.php?option=com _content&task=view&id=53&Itemid=122.*

2. Joel Andreas, *Addicted to War: Why the U.S. Can't Kick Militarism* (Oakland, CA: AK Press, 2003), and Martin Cerri, "Invasiones de EEUU a América Latina," in *Latinoamérica Mundial,* 2005, 32–33.

3. See, for instance, United Nations University and Institute for Development Economics Research study, *The World Distribution of Household Wealth,* December 2006, 63. When you compare U.S. consumption against the poorer half of the world's population, the consumption inequities grow dramatically.

4. See World Resources Institute, EarthTrends: The Environmental Information Portal, "Resource Consumption, 2005," *http://earthtrends.wri.org/datatables/index .php?theme=6.*

5. John Perkins, *Confessions of an Economic Hit Man* (New York: Penguin, 2005), 141–45. See also Grandin, *Empire's Workshop.*

6. Operation Condor was a concerted effort by South American dictators from a variety of countries working together to eliminate political opposition through state terrorism, assassinations, torture, and disappearances with U.S. assistance and advice.

7. Since NAFTA was signed with Mexico in 1994, the result has been a three-fold increase in migration of the rural and urban poor northward.

8. *Chicago Tribune,* May 15, 2006. *http://newsblogs.chicagotribune.com/news_ theswamp/2006/05/durbin_bring_ir.html.*

9. See *Pulling Apart,* published by the Center for Budget and Policy Priorities and the Economic Policy Institute, at *www.epinet.org/studies/pulling06/pulling_apart_ 2006.pdf.*

10. For the recent rise in U.S. infant mortality, see the report "America's Health State: State Health Rankings released at the 132nd Annual Meeting of the American Public Health Association," reported at Medscape Today; see *www.medscape.com/viewarticle/493512.* See U.S. Census Bureau web site for stagnant U.S poverty rates: *www.census.gov.*

7. Culture and Violence

1. For more on this see René Girard's books on the cultural and philosophical roots of violence.

2. Ward Churchill, *Indians Are Us: Culture and Genocide in Native North America* (Monroe, ME: Common Courage Press, 1993).

3. Bartolomé de Las Casas, *A Brief History of the Destruction of the Indies,* and Michael D. Coe, Dean R. Snow, and Elizabeth P. Benson, *Atlas of Ancient America* (New York: Facts on File, 1986).

4. Michael Clodfelter, *Warfare and Armed Conflict: A Statistical Reference to Casualty and Other Figures,* 2 vols. (Jefferson, NC: McFarland, 1992).

5. See ibid. See also Melvin Small and J. David Singer, *Resort to Arms: International and Civil Wars 1816–1980* (Beverly Hills, CA: Sage Publications, 1982); Max Boot, *The Savage Wars of Peace: Small Wars and the Rise of American Power,* reprint edition (New York: Basic Books, 2003).

6. Henry Graff, *American Imperialism and the Philippine Insurrection* (Boston: Little, Brown, 1969).

7. *Encyclopaedia Britannica,* 15th ed., 1992.

8. J. Keegan, ed., *Atlas of the Second World War* (London: Times Books/Guild Publishing, 1989).

9. Hiroshima: 88,800; Nagasaki: 73,884. From the Chugoku, "Actual Status Survey of Atomic Bomb Survivors," Shimburu, August 5, 1999, Nagasaki Atomic Bomb Museum, Nagasaki, Japan.

10. South Korean military deaths: 225,784; South Korean civilian deaths: 373,500; South Korean missing: 387,740; North Korean military deaths: 294,151; North Korean civilian deaths: 406,000; North Korean missing: 680,000. Andrew Nahm, *Historical Dictionary of the Republic of Korea* (Lanham, MD: Scarecrow Press, 1993).

11. South Vietnamese military deaths: 223,748; South Vietnamese civilian deaths: 300,000; North Vietnamese military deaths: 666,000; North Vietnamese civilian deaths: 65,000. Harry Summers, *Vietnam War Almanac* (San Francisco: Presidio Press, 1999). See *www.unknownnews.net/casualties.html.*

12. Noam Chomsky, *Deterring Democracy* (New York: Hill and Wang, 1992).

13. Iraq Police/Military: 4,143 + Iraq Civilian: 28,473; Iraq Coalition Casualty Count, *http://icasualties.org/,* February 21, 2006; see also Iraq Body Count, *www.iraqbodycount.net,* February 21, 2006.

14. *www.kucinich.house.gov/UploadedFiles/int3.pdf.*

15. Jared Diamond, *Guns, Germs, and Steel: The Fates of Human Societies* (New York: W. W. Norton, 1997, 1999).

16. See, for instance, "Washington no cree en lágrimas," *El Progreso*, March 30, 2003. U.S television networks do not air these images, but they appear to the rest of the world. This does not represent a propaganda attack by the world media community against the United States. Rather it represents a form of media censorship within the United States.

17. For more on this strain of neoconservative thought and its relationship to Christian fundamentalism see especially Greg Grandin, *Empire's Workshop: Latin America, the United States, and the Rise of the New Imperialism* (New York: Metropolitan Books, 2006), chapter 4, "Bringing It All Back Home: The Politics of the New Imperialism."

18. See, for instance, Diarmuid O'Murchu, *Evolutionary Faith: Rediscovering God in Our Great Story* (Maryknoll, NY: Orbis Books, 2002).

19. Martinillo, quoted in Francisco Martín Moreno, *México mutilado* (Miami: Alfaguara/Santillana USA, 2004).

20. In "La responsabilidad del pueblo de Estados Unidos por Gilberto López y Rivas," *La Jornada de México*, December 2005. Posted at *www.elcorreo.eu.org/esp/article.php3?id_article=6163*.

8. Mary's Paradox

1. At the time of this writing, a sudden increase in the price of corn and all corn-related food products has taken place due to a new market for corn-based bio-fuels and to hoarding and price gouging by the same large conglomerates that have been able to keep prices for corn (though not tortillas) so low for the past twelve years of NAFTA. The connection between the low corn prices that have forced Mexican farmers off the land and the high food prices that presently threaten Mexicans with hunger is an unregulated market where prices are at the mercy of corporate giants that manipulate prices for their own purposes.

2. During the first twelve years of NAFTA this manipulation of low prices destroyed Mexican corn production, causing in the state of Nayarit alone a reduction from 130,000 hectares planted to only 12,000 in 2006. Now representatives of Cargill and Monsanto in Mexico use these reductions as proof that Mexico does not have the capacity to produce its corn needs and therefore to avoid scarcities and hunger should import more foreign corn, including genetically modified varieties at new high prices.

9. The Organizing Poor and Their Advocates

1. The term "Second World Superpower" began to be used about 2003.

2. At *www.cristianosporlapaz.info*.

3. A concept stimulated by Nobel Peace Prize recipient Professor Muhammad Yunus and his Grameen Bank initiative in Bangladesh.

4. World Social Forum: *www.forumsocialmundial.org.br*.

5. One Web-based report indicated that 10,000 gathered in Mali. *http://english.pravda.ru/world/africa/23-01-2006/9542-mali-0*, and Wikipedia reports attendance

at the 2007 World Social Forum in Nairobi at 66,000 people from 110 countries. *http://en.wikipedia.org/wiki/World_social_forum.*

6. From the WSF web site: *www.forumsocialmundial.org.br/main.php?id_menu =19&cd_language=2.*

7. See a limited list of such international citizens' organizations in appendix A.

8. Food and Agriculture Organization of the United Nations, Trade Reforms and Food Security, *www.fao.org/DOCREP/005/Y4671E/y4671e0e.htm#bm14.*

9. As mentioned above, in early 2007 corn prices rose, but food prices also rose out of all proportion to the rise in grain prices as foreign and Mexican monopolies took hoarded grains and manipulated prices of tortillas and other corn-related foods, creating a food crisis for the Mexican populace.

10. For the full text of a sample declaration of the movement see appendix B, Declaration of the Fourth Mesoamerican Forum.

11. Declaración del Tercer Foro Contra el Plan Puebla Panama.

12. Tina Rosenberg, "The Free Trade Fix," *New York Times Magazine,* August 18, 2002.

13. See, for instance, Enrique Davila, Georgina Kessel, and Santiago Levy, *El sur también existe: Un ensayo sobre el desarrollo regional de México,* July 19, 2002, which presents a clear outline of this train of thought.

14. Declaración del Primer Foro Contra El Plan Puebla Panama.

15. See the video *Global Banquet,* produced by Maryknoll productions, available at *www.maryknoll.org.*

16. Ibid.

17. From Evo Morales's presidential inaugural address in *La Jornada de México,* January 26, 2006.

18. "Global Trends 2020 — Mapping the Global Future." See *www.dni.gov/nic/ NIC_2020_project.html.*

19. Ibid.

20. Americas Policy, International Relations Center, October 11, 2004. See online *www.americaspolicy.org.*

10. Exchanging Universes

1. Diarmuid O'Murchu, *Evolutionary Faith: Rediscovering God in Our Great Story* (Maryknoll, NY: Orbis Books, 2004), 200ff.

2. There has been considerable controversy regarding Chief Seattle's actual words; see *http://thegoldweb.com/voices/seattle.htm.* We quote the popular version here.

3. O'Murchu, *Evolutionary Faith,* 140.

4. Jared Diamond, *Collapse: How Societies Choose to Fail or Succeed* (New York: Viking Books, 2005), 155.

11. A Special Time of Hope

1. Our purpose in this book is to advance a reflection toward a national change of heart, a new consciousness with which to face challenges of the very different kind of future that awaits us. We will leave detailed political policies and directions that can flow from this new consciousness to those more experienced in political and policy analysis.

2. Diarmuid O'Murchu, *Evolutionary Faith: Rediscovering God in Our Great Story* (Maryknoll, NY: Orbis Books, 2004), 200ff.

3. See Angus Wright, *The Death of Ramón González* (Austin: University of Texas Press, 2005).

4. Jim Wallis, *God's Politics: Why the Right Gets It Wrong and the Left Doesn't Get It* (New York: HarperCollins, 2005), 280.

5. From talks by Ivette Perfecto at Yale International Workshop, "Food Sovereignty, Conservation, and Social Movements for Sustainable Agriculture in the Americas," August 15–17, 2004, Yale University School of Forestry and Environmental Studies, *perfecto@umich.edu*.

6. O'Murchu, *Evolutionary Faith*, 148.

12. Happiness and a Sustainable World

1. Other authors have traced a relationship between the affluence of our American society and the incidence of chemical and behavioral addictions. For more on this see Anne Wilson Shaef and Dianne Fassel, *The Addictive Organization: Why We Overwork, Cover Up, Pick Up the Pieces, Please the Boss, and Perpetuate Sick Organizations* (New York: HarperCollins, 1990).

2. See online *www.washingtonmonthly.com/features/2003/0310.wallace-wells2.html*. For the complete text of Bush's address see *www.whitehouse.gov/news/releases/2001/09/20010920-8.html*.

3. George Kennan, ex-U.S. State Department policy planning staff chief, Document PPS23, February 24, 1948.

4. As reported by David Brooks, "Oligarcas súper ricos, Los únicos beneficiados en la economía de EU," *La Jornada de México,* March 3, 2006.

5. Stephen Hicken, Hector Medina, and Nora Petersen, *Reading the Signs of the Times/Intrepretando los señales de los tiempos* (San Jose, CA: Resource Publications, 2001).

6. Tom Barry et al., *A Global Good Neighbor Ethic for International Relations,* International Relations Center/Foreign Policy in Focus Special Report, May 2005, 5, *www.irc-online.org/content/ggn/0505ggn.php.*

7. Ibid., 9.

8. Ibid., 26.

9. Available at *www.globalgoodneighbor.org.*

Glossary

arroyo: a small steep-sided watercourse or gulch with a nearly flat floor; usually dry except after heavy rains.

atole: a thick, corn-based hot drink.

bienes comunales: a term used by rural Oaxacan municipal governments to define all of the commonly owned property and land within the municipal boundaries.

calenda: a small parade.

campesinos: rural small farmers. The name usually refers also to the culture and lifestyle of these peoples.

cargos: a system of nonpaid, full- or part-time responsibilities that members of indigenous communities must be willing to undertake several times over the course of their adult lifetimes as an expression of their local indigenous citizenship.

castillo: a large framework made to resemble, for example, a castle, a bull, the Virgen of Guadalupe covered with fireworks. When lit, a *castillo* ignites by parts in a progression. Every major village fiesta includes the lighting of a *castillo*.

coa: a tool for planting corn used in the Mixteca Alta. It is a long wooden stick with a shovel-like tool on one end and a sharp, metal-tipped point on the other.

cohetero: persons who make fireworks displays.

elite: a leguminous species of alder tree that takes rapidly in the eroded soils of the Mixteca Alta of Oaxaca state.

guelaguetza: guelaguetza: an expression of mutuality in relationship in which you receive a gift, offering, or assistance from your neighbor and are expected to reciprocate. More than simply "give and take," guelaguetza creates security, balance, and dignity in relationships. Presently it also refers to the annual statewide festival held in the capital city on a mountainside held sacred among Zapotec peoples.

gueza: The Mixtec word for *guelaguetza*.

mayordomia, mayordomo: the principal host of a town festival is called a *mayordomo*. The action and event of hosting the event is a *mayordomia*. Indigenous peoples consider the role of *mayordomo* a great honor, though it may entail enormous costs. Those charged with paying for one portion of a major festival (such as the sound system, flowers, or *mescal*) are likewise called *mayordomos*.

mestizo: people of both Spanish and Indigenous descent. Most Mexicans are mestizo.

milpa: a term commonly used for a field of corn, but more accurately it refers to a field of the traditional companion plants, corn, beans, and squash, which have been the staples of the Mexican diet for centuries.

mole: a famous Oaxacan sauce, pronounced MO-lay, and made of almost thirty ingredients including chocolate, peanuts, and chile.

posole: a hearty corn-based soup.

quelites: a variety of edible green leafy plant that grows on its own in and around cultivated fields. It constitutes a rich nutritional source of the campesino diet.

tamales: a wrap of chicken, mole, chile, or sauce in a corn-based paste. The tamale is wrapped in a banana leaf or corn husk and boiled.

teocintle: common ancestor of the many strains and varieties of the world's corn.

tepache: a lightly fermented local drink of pineapple and sugar cane.

tequio: the common work projects the villagers commit themselves to as part of their community obligations.

tlayuda: a large delicious tortilla covered with various toppings and sauces.

Index

185

Phil Dahl-Bredine (right), born in Kansas City, Missouri, is married and has seven adult children. He and his wife, Kathy, live in the village of San Isidro, Tilantongo, in the Mixteca Alta of Oaxaca. They both have worked almost seven years with indigenous villages as part of their work with the Maryknoll Lay Missioner Association. Phil has an M.A. in Philosophy from Northwestern University and has worked for decades with Catholic Worker communities in Chicago, farmed in Burlington, Wisconsin, and worked more than twenty years with projects in the Chicano community of southern New Mexico.

Stephen Hicken has dedicated twenty-five years to work both in the United States and Latin America in the field of addressing poverty, strengthening human rights, and building international solidarity. He and his wife, Mary, have four children. He now lives in Castro Valley, California, and is starting an organization to link immigrants with development projects in their communities of origin.